MW01490283

Stay Salty

STORIES OF FAITH & HOPE

CAV WOMEN'S DEVOTIONS

WESTBOW
PRESS®
A DIVISION OF THOMAS NELSON
& ZONDERVAN

WestBow Press books may be ordered through booksellers or by contacting:

WestBow Press
A Division of Thomas Nelson & Zondervan
1663 Liberty Drive
Bloomington, IN 47403
www.westbowpress.com
844-714-3454

ISBN: 979-8-3850-0060-9 (sc)
ISBN: 979-8-3850-0062-3 (hc)
ISBN: 979-8-3850-0061-6 (e)

Library of Congress Control Number: 2023911210

Print information available on the last page.

WestBow Press rev. date: 06/28/2023

Dedicated to Sue Lewis and Kelli Ragsdale
for your leadership, authenticity and love
of faith, family and friendship.
You are examples to all of a Christ-centered life.

Church at Viera

GOD HAS A PLAN

For I know the plans I have for you, they are plans for good and not for disaster, to give you a future and a hope. In those days when you pray, I will listen. If you look for me wholeheartedly, you will find me. I will be found by you."

JEREMIAH 29:11-13 (NEW LIVING TRANSLATION)

S ome of us have lived long enough to have had times where we've been able to look back and think, "Oh that's why God did that!" Sometimes we've not had the privilege of knowing for a long time what that plan is, and there are some things we may never know this side of heaven. One thing that I know for sure is that God always has a plan. He is continually writing our stories, sometimes despite our choices! One of the foundations of my walk with the Lord has been believing that God always has a plan. His timing might not be our timing, but it's always the perfect time!

When my daughter Jessica showed me an ultrasound picture early in her second pregnancy, I was expecting to see one tiny little blob of a life just beginning to develop. When I took a second look, I was shocked to see three blobs. In my mind I thought, "Is this what I think it is?" There were three tiny little lives living inside the womb of my precious daughter! How could this be? God what in the world are you thinking? Triplets?

As I began to process what this would mean for her and her little family, the enormity of it began to unfold in my mind - this is going to change everything in our whole family! That still, small voice of the Holy Spirit kept whispering, "God has a plan." I was full of fear for my own child and how this would affect her but still the whisper came, "God has a plan."

Jeremiah 29:11 says, "For I know the plans I have for you,' says the Lord. They are plans for good and not for disaster, to give you a future and a hope. In those days when you pray, I will listen. If you look for me wholeheartedly, you will find me. I will be found by you."

I love the last part of that verse where He promises us that if we look for Him we will find Him.

> When we lose someone we love...
> We will find him! He has a plan!
> When a child that we have loved
> and nurtured goes astray...
> We will find him! He has a plan!
> When we are betrayed ...
> We will find him! He has a plan!
> When we are disappointed...
> We will find him! He has a plan!
> When things happen that we don't understand...
> We will find him! He has a plan!

I could go on and on as we all have situations in life that are just, well, hard. My dad passed away at the age of 66 after suffering terribly with cancer eating his body away. I can remember sitting by his deathbed and praying God, I don't understand why this is happening, but I do trust your plan. His whole plan in that hasn't yet been revealed to me, but I do see some of how God has worked through it. We might not always see the plan, but God is always working and we can trust in Him and His Word.

Psalm 33:11 NLT says, "But the Lord's plans stand firm forever; his intentions can never be shaken."

Believing in His plan isn't always easy! There can be times when it will take every ounce of faith you have to believe there is a plan but keep pressing on and trusting! I have found through many of my own fumblings in faith that His plans and His ways are always intentional, and HE IS FOR US!

"We put our hope in the Lord. He is our help and our shield. In him our hearts rejoice, for we trust in his holy name. Let your unfailing love surround us, Lord, for our hope is in you alone," Psalm 33:20-22 NLT,

I'm grateful to sing on our worship team. Musical worship is one of my greatest passions and I think often about the lyrics we sing. Some of the songs we sing resonate with this idea of trusting God's plan. I love these lyrics from the song by Elevation Worship, Give Me Faith:

> GIVE ME FAITH to trust what you say.
> That you're good and your love is great...
> I may be weak but Your Spirit's strong in me,
> my flesh may fail but my God You never will!

Kelli Ragsdale

GOD THINGS

"I can do all things through Christ who strengthens me."

PHILIPPIANS 4:13 (NEW KING JAMES VERSION)

I attended church as a child and into my teens. Then, I wandered. In my early twenties, I had a job at an aircraft instrument repair shop but when things became difficult there, I left. I read the job postings at the local state employment office, and I applied for a job that I clearly qualified for at an Air Force station, but I was not hired.

Six months later, I was working as a receptionist at a local manufacturing plant when I got a phone call with a job offer. It was definitely a "God thing" because I didn't know anyone there or have any connections. I accepted the job. I would now be working on the Air Force Titan program for an independent contractor. My job involved issuing and delivering tools, parts and test equipment to work sites used to assemble the Titan missile solid rocket motors. I enjoyed this kind of work, so I felt truly blessed!

Seventeen years later, the Air Force Titan program was winding down and I began to realize I would be laid off when the work there was finished. A year later, it happened. I then decided to use my unemployment benefits to attend the local community college full time. As my unemployment benefits ran out, I prayed about my next job. I was now attending church weekly and was very close to God. My prayer was that my next job would be in an office environment after having worked in a warehouse atmosphere for eighteen years.

Six months later, I found a job posting with Northrop Grumman

Corporation. I met the requirements with my prior work experience, and I was hired. God answered my prayers. It was another stupendous "God thing," without a doubt. With God, there are no coincidences.

During the years that I had those two jobs, I had many challenges in life—a divorce, forty-seven years of marriage, becoming a stepmother, raising four children in a blended family while working full time, dealing with troubled stepsons, and the deaths of my two brothers and my parents. All of this was complicated by the fact that I have been an introvert my whole life. But God was with me. I am humbled that God has given me opportunities to help others—helping a child who is struggling to read, teaching a young mom how to use a sewing machine, or giving a hug to a hurting woman. The hurting woman I hugged was someone I met at the gym. The next time I saw her there, she told me how much that hug meant to her. I responded, "That wasn't me, that was a 'God thing.'"

When my tenants were moving from my rental home, God prompted me to rent it to a wonderful godly lady from my church. Now, I am overjoyed that she is at home there and no longer needs to be concerned and stressed about the upkeep on her house. There it is again, a "God thing."

At this time in my life, I am getting to know more about God through prayer, attending church and Bible study, and listening to Christian music. I am blessed to feel closer to Him and to understand what the Holy Spirit is teaching me. Jesus Christ is my world, my life. I wouldn't trade anything for the joy and peace He has given me.

Mary Weldon

THE WILL OF GOD

"Rejoice always, pray without ceasing, give thanks in all circumstances; for this is the will of God in Christ Jesus for you."

I Thessalonians 5:16–18 (English Standard Version)

I wake with a startling jump. A rush of adrenaline surges through my body as my heart begins to race. "Was it just a dream?" I ask myself with hopeful expectations. My husband's strong and loving arms hold me close, giving me warmth, peace, and comfort. The damp puddle of tears on my pillow reminds me, to my horror, that this was not a dream.

My body starts to quiver, and unrelenting tears fall from my eyes as I recall receiving the phone call yesterday when my weeping husband told me our precious son, Patrick, had ended his life. I could not breathe. The worst fear of my entire life came true. I sobbed and cried out to God, as I knew the Lord wept over my husband and me when we heard of this tragedy.

In the stillness of the next morning, I quietly gasp and desperately try to hold back the guttural groans within my soul as I grieve the loss of my firstborn son. It feels as if a part of my very soul has been ripped from me. My body feels like a giant open wound, like my every nerve is exposed. Words falter to describe the intense agony a parent experiences over the death of his or her child.

I slowly reach to the nightstand to grab my Bible. I know I dare not let my feet touch the floor without first reading God's Word. I pray and beg God to help me through this terrifying nightmare. I had walked with God for over four decades and knew that it was only God who could heal me wholly. Over the years, the Lord has taught me that in every circumstance, we have the choice to complain or be grateful. God taught me to choose to be thankful, which had transformed my mind and given me abundant life in Him (John 10:10). Yet, this morning I am struggling.

"God, how can I be thankful—my son is gone! I just want to hold his hand again, smell his hair, listen to him share his heart with me. Death is horrific. What do I do, Lord?" Then I began searching— what is God's will in this circumstance? Interestingly, I discover there are only five places in the Bible where it specifically articulates the will of the Lord. God brings me to I Thessalonians 5:16–18 ESV.

"Rejoice always," (v. 16). God, how can I rejoice in the death of my son? God's still small voice speaks to my heart, reminding me that I have an incredible godly husband who loves me dearly and three wonderful living children who are my greatest blessings. "Okay, Lord Jesus, I will rejoice over these other amazing blessings you have given me."

"Pray without ceasing," (v. 17). Well, that was easy. I cannot stop praying. I am continually seeking God as I need Him for the air in my lungs. I desperately cry out to Him to take the next step, one foot in front of the other. I desperately need His help to minister and comfort my children and my husband.

"Give thanks in all circumstances," (v. 18). Oh Lord, how do I do this? I look around and see two of our grandchildren snuggled beside us. Our four grandchildren are so young, and they do not fully understand what has happened. They are playful, loving, and full of laughter. They bring joy to our hearts amid great grief. "Even in laughter, the heart may ache, and the end of joy may be grief," Proverbs 14:13 ESV. God gives me this verse as a smile creeps over my face while experiencing deep sadness. It is an incredible miracle that grief and joy can coexist in one's heart. "Okay Lord, I can do this. I will give thanks for these precious grandchildren you blessed us with. I will give thanks for how You lovingly care for us during this time of great sorrow."

"For this is the will of God in Christ Jesus for you," (v. 18). God has all the answers to our many questions. Often, we try to avoid pain: we hide it, ignore it, seek retail therapy, binge drink, or overmedicate ourselves through times of difficulty. These outlets damage and destroy us. God gives us Scripture to guide and direct us to live a healthy and abundant life in Him.

What about you? Who or what do you turn to when you are suffering or experience sadness? What will the consequences of that look like in five years? In ten years? After all, every decision we make today will have consequences that last for eternity.

In this life we will have suffering (John 16:33). Yet, this is not the end. Heaven is our home where suffering ceases. This was only made possible by God the Father when He willingly gave His only begotten Son, Jesus, to suffer the punishment of our sin, that we might be forgiven and saved through Him. God understands the pain of losing a child and He willingly gave His Son because He loves us so much! That is a love far beyond our comprehension.

The tears stop flowing from my eyes. I feel the warmth of the Lord fill my heart and soul. I still feel as if my entire body is a deep open wound, but God applies the salve of my family's love on my wound. Will you allow God to heal your wounds?

Harmony Charters

HE REMAINS FAITHFUL

"If we are faithless, he remains faithful, for he cannot disown himself."

II TIMOTHY 2:13 (NEW INTERNATIONAL VERSION)

I clearly remember as a small child the feeling of being in love with Jesus and in awe of God. Being blessed at an early age to attend church and to witness my parent's devotion to God supported the fact that God is love. Our church family lived by the principles Jesus taught in Matthew 18:4 NASB: "So whoever will humble himself like this child, he is the greatest in the kingdom of heaven." Exemplifying this verse, a member of our church family gifted me a beautiful handcrafted cross necklace when I was quite young. I cherished this cross for many years because, at the time, I valued and understood the sacrifice it represented.

The man who handcrafted this cross for me, spent many hours cutting, shaping, sanding, applying stain and lacquer, and tying the string of leather to make it a necklace. See, this man was a carpenter, just like Jesus. As a youth, it was inspiring to hear stories of Jesus as a carpenter and how his true work would be building His church. Scripture tells us, "Do not let your hearts be troubled. You believe in God; believe also in me. My Father's house has many rooms; if that were not so, would I have told you that I am going there to prepare a place for you?" John 14:1-2 NIV.

Unfortunately, several years later the cross was lost. I was also lost. My prior childlike perspective was overridden with the problems and temptations of this world. Instead of living for the Word, I was living for the world. This went on for almost thirty years but during this time the foundation of faith was not forgotten. Jesus was walking beside me protecting my family and me. By the standards of the world, I was living a good life, better than others, or so I thought. Fortunately, God knew my heart and my desire for Him.

When my husband decided it was in the best interest of our family to move, I wondered how leaving our adult children and my favorite town could be good for my family. Then I remembered the example set by my mother from Ephesians 5:22, wherein Paul says we must submit to our husbands. I trusted God's Word and submitted.

After our move, I realized why God brought our family here. God had a plan. We built a home, our children followed, we welcomed a grandchild and most importantly, we found a church. Little did we know that our new home would be in a neighborhood with faithful Christians. Now I could learn more about Jesus. Our neighbors began to witness to us about Jesus and I learned about His grace. I bought a Bible and attended Bible studies. I was inspired by one simple but powerful verse: "Therefore, there is now no condemnation for those who are in Christ Jesus," Romans 8:1 NIV.

Seven years after we moved to our new neighborhood, I accepted Jesus as my Savior and showed my obedience to Him by being baptized. God led me to this town and to His people. We have to listen to His calling and have faith in His Word and that's why this verse means so much to me: "And we know that in all things God works for the good of those who love him, who have been called according to his purpose," Romans 8:28 NIV.

Shortly after my baptism my mother returned the cross necklace to me. It was never lost but instead it was waiting for me to find Jesus. What started out as a mustard seed of faith flourished into faith so deep and rich that I am now a disciple of Jesus.

"Lord, you are my God; I will exalt you and praise your name, for in perfect faithfulness you have done wonderful things, things planned long ago," Isaiah 25:1 NIV.

Michelle Saunders

ACCOUNTABILITY IN THE HOME

"Iron sharpens iron, and one man sharpens another."

PROVERBS 27:17 (ENGLISH STANDARD VERSION)

D id you read that passage and think, wait, I thought this was a women's devotional? This much quoted verse is associated often with Men's ministry. In many churches I have been a part of, it was even the theme of their Men's ministry. For that reason, it's been a verse that I've often overlooked. Recently I was listening to a sermon by Texas pastor, Matt Chandler. He mentioned this verse and encouraged that as believers, we should all take this verse to heart. I began to think about who I am called to sharpen, why it's so important and how I can do this.

Who am I to be sharpening? For iron to sharpen iron, it must be in close proximity. For me, the people in closest proximity to me are my family members—my husband and children. I have an accountability partner I meet with each week and while I am sharpening her and she me, yet my husband and family are in the closest proximity. They have been placed in my life by the Lord and I believe He has uniquely gifted me to speak truth to them and they to me. It is hard to keep secrets when you live in the same house. We see each other's good and bad days. We are together through successes and failures. I try to be as honest as I can with my accountability partner but there are times I might not share everything or share the full extent of what is happening. My husband sees it all and I want him to call me out when I need it just as much as I want his encouragement when I am doing well. With my children, when I see them walking down a path that is not following Christ, I want to encourage them and help them seek Truth. I also want them to know that I am not without struggles and that they can question me if they feel I am not honoring Christ in the things I say and do.

Why is this so important? God's Word says, "Your adversary the devil prowls around like a roaring lion, seeking someone to devour," 1 Peter 5:8 ESV. Every day we are in a battle. Satan wants to tempt us, to lure us away so he can destroy us. The picture I get from this verse is like those National Geographic specials where there is a herd of antelopes grazing peacefully and a lion begins to stalk them. The lion does not typically attack the whole herd. It begins to try to separate one weak antelope from the herd to devour. Satan is the same. When we are together, encouraging each other in our walk, pointing out weakness that Satan could exploit, praying for each other, spurring one another on in the pursuit of holiness, we are going to be much harder for Satan to take down or devour.

How do I sharpen the iron that is my family? It is not by looking for every mistake or failure. We will not win them over by nagging or criticizing them. Who wants to be vulnerable and take corrections from someone like that? Honestly, it starts with humility—giving them a chance to see where I struggle, confessing when I have blown it, and then asking for their forgiveness. By asking them to lift me up in prayer, I will not fall victim to Satan's schemes in the future. By being humble and teachable myself, I'm inviting them to help me become who God wants me to be—to be used for His glory. In doing that, my hope and prayer is that I can do the same for them.

"But exhort one another every day, as long as it is called 'today' that none of you may be hardened by the deceitfulness of sin" Hebrews 3:13 NIV.

Heather Leathers

EVERY GIRL NEEDS HER DAD

"Train up a child in the way he should go; even when he is old he will not depart from it."

PROVERBS 22:6 (ENGLISH STANDARD VERSION)

When I was in high school, a guest speaker came and spoke at our assembly about the importance of a dad in every girl's life. He taught us that anyone can be a father, but it takes a special person to be a dad. It has been found that there are benefits for girls with strong bonds with their dad, including more confidence, higher education, and better relationships in her life. A good dad is a provider, encourager, protector, and a devoted family man. The speaker said that girls who have a strong bond with their dad are happier and are less likely to feel the need to go looking to fill that gap with multiple boyfriends or bad boys.

That message always stuck with me. At the time, it made me realize how blessed I was that I had an amazing dad. I went home that day and thanked him for being a great dad. Girls need a dad to teach them "Dad" things, but more importantly to teach them their worth, and how they deserve to be loved and treated. "Train up a child in the way he should go; even when he is old he will not depart from it," Proverbs 22:6 ESV.

I have been blessed to have a close relationship with my father, as a young girl and now as an adult. He has always been there to listen, give advice, help me whenever I needed help, and he has always put his family first. He has been a great role model to me and to my two

13

girls. I have also been blessed to have met and married a man who is a wonderful husband to me and father to our two girls. My girls are blessed to have their father and grandfather to speak into their lives.

Not every girl is fortunate enough to have their biological father in their lives, but he is not the only one who can be a dad to them. A girl's dad can be a stepdad, an adoptive dad, a grandfather, an uncle, or a close family friend. No matter what a girl's situation is, there is one dad that any girl can always count on- that is our Heavenly Father. He is constant and ready to provide you with unconditional love, He tells you that you are worthy, and if you accept His love in return, He calls you daughter. "And I will be a father to you, and you shall be sons and daughters to me, says the Lord Almighty," 2 Corinthians 6:18 ESV. How amazing is that!

Stephanie Frisbee

Beach 2023 - Photo credit: Bernadette Skipper

MAKE THE MOST OF YOUR TIME

"Look carefully then how you walk, not as unwise men but as wise,
making the best use of the time, because the days are evil. Therefore, do
not be foolish,
but understand what the will of the Lord is."

EPHESIANS 5:15-17 (ENGLISH STANDARD VERSION)

I had coffee yesterday with a very dear friend. We love to encourage each other to have a "purpose driven life" and to use the gifts that God gave us to further His kingdom. It is always a special time of "girl talk." We're both doers and achievers, so encouraging each other to get out and DO is exciting for us. She happened to mention that she probably has about two decades left in her life. A little over twenty-two years to reach others for Christ and teach her passion, which is developing a meaningful prayer life.

Deep inside I'm thinking—"Whoa girl! ONLY twenty-two more years." I didn't say that to her, but right away I'm thinking—"Wow, that is not much time in our lives."

The words from Ephesians 5 popped out at me: "Make the best use of the time." I have been very blessed to travel the world, hike the Grand Canyon, see the powerful Niagara Falls, walk the Great Wall, teach children how to swim, bring three children into this world, multi-task with the best, and be married for over thirty years to the same man!

But maybe I haven't made the most of my time in terms of how God wants me to use my life. Maybe too much of my time has been spent on me and my family's hopes and dreams. How do you spend your time? How do you think God wants us to make the most of the time?

For me, in this season of my life, I don't go anywhere until I have a quiet time with God and let Him teach me from His Word. I've started to be more alert—to pray more fervently, and to walk more slowly in order to notice people in need, to care for the poor, and to cultivate deeper friendships. While I am in the grocery store, I try to observe who might need extra encouragement that day. I ask God to show me who He has put in my path to share my faith with, even if it means being late to spin class or yoga. Maybe there is a co-worker in your midst who could use some Godly encouragement this day!

My prayer is this—let us be wise and not foolish and make the most of our time while here on your precious earth, oh Lord!

Leslie Berens

BIBLICAL SELF LOVE

"Love the Lord your God with all your heart and with all your soul and with all your mind. This is the first and greatest commandment. And the second is like it: 'Love your neighbor as yourself.'"

MATTHEW 22:37-39 (NEW INTERNATIONAL VERSION)

If you grew up in the church, you may be familiar with Philippians 2:3 NIV which instructs believers to, "Do nothing out of selfish ambition or vain conceit. Rather, in humility, value others above yourselves." This verse has been cited as a warning against love of self. Yet, is love of self the same thing as self-love?

Love of self can be seen when a person is focused on herself at the expense of others. Love of self is evidenced by a "more about me" and "less about others" attitude and undesirable behaviors that result from that attitude. II Timothy 3:2 NIV warns us, "People will be lovers of themselves." Now consider the concept of "self-love." Sometimes "self-love" in our society is interpreted as self-care which at times can be associated with self-indulgence. But biblical self-love looks like something entirely different.

When you are unsure, where do you turn? Christians turn to Scripture. In Matthew 22:37-39, Jesus defines the greatest commandments—to love God with all of our heart, soul and mind and to love your neighbor as yourself. The focus of this verse is to love God and others, so what then is biblical self-love?

Biblical self-love is knowing who we are in Christ. It is being grounded in the knowledge that we are His handiwork. It is being good stewards of what has been given to us: our bodies, our gifts, our talents, and our testimonies. Biblical self-love refers to the manner in which we "treat" ourselves. God wants us to treat ourselves with the love, tenderness, and respect that we would treat something that is of great value. This includes how we care for our body, the type of language we use when we are speaking of ourselves, and what we expose ourselves to.

We are practicing biblical self L.O.V.E. when we practice self-care, self-control, self-compassion, and self-acceptance. As God fearing women, when we are loving ourselves, we are encouraged to:

L - Listen to our body and care for it through physical, emotional and intellectual self-care, movement and nourishment. I Corinthians 6:19 tells us, "Your bodies are temples of the Holy Spirit."

O - Observe our environment; practice "self-control"; be mindful of the people, places and things we are exposed to. For there are many things in this world that can distract us and move us away from God. When we are vigilant, we guard our hearts and draw near to Him. "Above all else, guard your heart," Proverbs 4:23 NIV. "Pay attention to and turn your ear to the sayings of the wise," Proverbs 22:17 NIV.

V – Value our story and the trials that make up our testimony. Practice "self-compassion" and release the burden of shame. Those who believe in Him are a new creation and without shame. "I sought the LORD, and he answered me; he delivered me from all my fears. Those who look to him are radiant; their faces are never covered with shame," Psalm 34:4-5 NIV. Rejoice that no matter where you have been, God has never been far away. He has walked alongside and sheltered you. Your story is your testimony and is worth sharing.

E – Embrace your unique gifts, practice self-acceptance and resist the urge to compare oneself to others. When we focus on what others have, envy and discontentment creep in. Instead, walk in the knowledge and understanding that we are God's handiwork, created with intention for His purpose: "We have different gifts, according to the grace given to each of us," Romans 12:6 NIV. Embrace your gifts and use them to glorify God.

Biblical self-love is love that reflects God's love, because He loved us first. Sister, as you move into this day, I pray that you walk clothed in God's love—let His love flow through you and pour out of you.

Tiffanie Trudeau

THE COMPARISON GAME

"My command is this: Love each other as I have loved you."

JOHN 15:12 (NEW INTERNATIONAL VERSION)

Years ago a good friend said to me, "You are a daughter of The King!" I was hearing this for the first time and WOW! I will never forget it. I had never considered this before and it made me consider how amazing God truly is and how much He truly loves me. I often share this with other women to remind them who they are, and whose they are and how fearfully and wonderfully they were made. I am a child of The King, you are a child of The King and we are sisters and brothers in Christ. God created each of us individually, with our own calling, to be the hands and feet of Jesus. Each of us has unique talents and gifts to contribute which include the fruits of the Spirit—love, joy, peace, patience, kindness, goodness, faithfulness, gentleness, and self-control.

I used to think that because of my strong commitment to Christ I could always love others, especially my brothers and sisters in Christ. But I began to realize that instead of loving others, I was constantly comparing and competing with them in my head and heart. I struggled when others received accolades. I would tear down instead of build up my family, other believers, those I worked with, and those I read about on social media. I thought of myself as humble, joyful and loving but that is not possible if I am playing the comparison game.

Competition can be a good thing when it brings out the best in you, but this was an ugly game of Monopoly, not a friendly game of Uno. I struggled with why and realized I could not love my neighbor if I did not love myself. I was hurting and broken on the inside. I did not believe who I was in Christ, therefore I was failing at loving others.

Loving myself and trusting in Christ is a total surrender to Him. Sometimes I have to surrender to Him daily. I choose Jesus each day, because I love who I am in Jesus. Competition and comparison are a losing battle. It feels dark. It takes you down a rabbit hole that leads to bitterness and envy.

By choosing J.O.Y. (Jesus, Others, Yourself) I am putting Jesus first, which enables me to put others ahead of myself. Life is not about my days being perfect, but knowing God has perfect love for me. Even on my worst days, I am loved and I can still love others. The only one who can take that from me, is me. It must be more of Jesus, less of me. I serve others because I truly love my sisters and brothers in Christ. I try to see the big picture, to look at situations from others perspectives and choose to love, encourage and serve them. I may not always be happy about a situation or the way my day is going but I find joy in knowing I am the daughter of The King, in knowing God has a calling for me. I am serving Him by loving others, not by comparing, not by competing, but by simply loving. We are called to love.

Monie Rosenberger

THE THREE HUNDRED

*"The Lord said to Gideon, 'With the three hundred men that lapped
I will save you and give the Midianites into your hands. Let all the
others go home.'"*

JUDGES 7:7 (NEW INTERNATIONAL VERSION)

I have grown to love looking for what God has to show me in the
stories of the Old Testament which go back to the beginning
of time. One story I have gleaned a lot from is the account
of Gideon in Judges 6–8. Instead of using the 32,000 men he had
available to fight against the Midianites who were oppressing the
Israelites, God wanted him to use only 300 men. God wanted the
Israelites to know the credit for victory was His. Their odds went
from 4:1 to 450:1. They were already outnumbered, now they were
ridiculously outnumbered. It doesn't matter to God; He can use any
number. His math is not our math.

As I was studying this story several years ago, I was fascinated by
how God used the 300 to win the battle. My husband and I were in
a bit of our own battle at the time. It was a financial battle—we had
more month left than we had money for. When your main source
of income is from commissions, trusting God is a key component.
Unsure how we would cover some expenses, one day I received a call
from a new friend of ours. She asked me if I would be home as she
had something she HAD to drop off. It sounded urgent! I told her
to come on over. She told me she was in a hurry and would not have
time even to get out of her car. I watched for her and ran out to the

driveway when she pulled in. She handed me an envelope without any explanation other than, "God told me to give this to you, and I didn't want to put it off for a minute." With that, she backed out of the driveway and was gone. Standing in front of my house, tears filled my eyes as I opened the small envelope and saw $300 cash. The tiny "post-it" note inside just said, "Hi Jeannie - Just felt led by the Lord to give you this. It's for you. Love ya!!" I was stunned! There was something very special about that number…300!

My husband was amazed as well. I had been telling him Gideon's story and how God used just 300 so that He could get the glory and there would be no mistake about WHO won the victory. We realized God had provided for us and WHO was in control. When God took it down from 32,000 men to 300, there would be no mistake about WHO was in control. What a blessing that God would care enough to prompt a person, out of the blue, to put some money in an envelope that would assist us to cover a need. What a blessing that God would also use the specific amount to REMIND us that He would take care of us and that He was the one in control.

It is important to be in the Word of God daily. Both the New Testament and the Old Testament have much we can learn from. God can use what we read there to touch our hearts, and speak to us in ways no other book can. Had I not been studying the story of Gideon, the gift we received would have still helped us, but we would not have tied it to the message God wanted to send us.

Later, I thanked my friend and told her what a blessing from God her gift had been. When I told her about studying Gideon and how God used that to send us a message, she was overjoyed and praised the Lord and gave him Glory! You see, It is awesome to allow the Lord to use you to be a blessing to someone even when you don't understand why you are doing it. Our obedience brings true joy and glory to God!

The story of Gideon is also a reminder of how God sees us differently than we see ourselves. Gideon was just a regular guy, actually the "least" in his family—but God saw him as a mighty warrior (Judges 6:12). The story of Gideon is also a reminder of

God's patience. God was repeatedly patient and understanding when Gideon puts the fleece out to test Him, not once but twice! (Judges 6:36–40) One of my favorite parts of the story is when God tells Gideon if he is afraid, to go listen to some of the Midianites and he will be encouraged. Wow! Was he ever encouraged! Read Judges 7:9–15 to be encouraged also.

God delights in using regular people who may be a little unsure and a little afraid. God encourages people when He uses them. And, like Gideon, we need to listen to God, trust Him, and follow through to bring God the glory.

The number 300 will always remind me that God is in control!

Jeannie Amaral

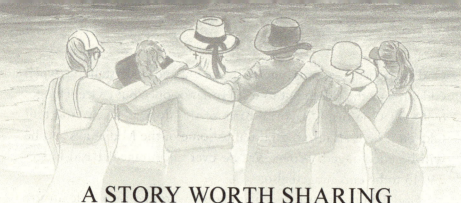

A STORY WORTH SHARING

"After that whole generation had been gathered to their ancestors,
another generation grew up who knew neither the LORD nor what He
had done for Israel."

———————

JUDGES 2:10, NIV

O ur God is a God of miracles, and He is the same God yesterday, as today and tomorrow. Stories of His miracles have been recorded, scribbled on pages, and shared at bedtime. His miracles have touched the lives of people from thousands of years ago, through to my parent's generation. And if I am to be truthful, I could look back forty years, twenty months, ten days, and sometimes just a moment ago in my own life and be able to point out exactly where and when God sprinkled down a few miracles. Sometimes, a miracle is evident, and in that moment, I lift my hands as I fall to my knees in praise! Other times it may take days, months, or even years for the story to unfold and my heart to reflect back before a miracle becomes visible to me. Nevertheless, I know with confidence that my life has been touched by the hand of God, and the stories of His miracles have been etched on my heart.

But now, I stand in the present, and I discover that standing in the present can be one of the most challenging places to stand. I may have heard, seen and even experienced His miracles in the past, while hoping for His goodness to be revealed in the future, but what about the now? Standing in the now is where I experience and where I feel. Now is where He is working, and where I can take notice. I take note of the pain, the weariness, the uncertainty, the fear, the anticipation, the excitement, and the joy. Whatever it might be, I take note.

And then, inspired by past scribbles on paper and etchings on my heart I create a written testament of God's miracles in my life, my testimony. It is a story unique to me, a story that I have been gifted by my Father. It is a story that I once believed belonged solely to me, like a precious journal to which I was the only one to hold a key. And because it contained my life's secrets, I held it ever so close to my heart with a grip so tight, I was determined to never let go. But then God....

Judges 2:10 reveals, "After that whole generation had been gathered to their ancestors, another generation grew up who knew neither the LORD nor what He had done for Israel."

With the Holy Spirit beginning to soften my heart, only then did I choose to slowly loosen my grip and lift my open palms to the Lord, understanding that each miracle I had made not of, no matter how big or small, was actually a part of His story!

If I choose not to share that journal revealing the miracles of love and grace and forgiveness and redemption that I have had the blessing to experience in my life, then who will share them? How will my children and my children's children come to know God's miracles of past and present if I choose not to share those stories? Who will tell them of the God of miracles?

Those stories, those testaments, reveal the truth that our God of past miracles is presently working in and through us to gather His people together, that we might spend eternity in His loving presence. Therefore, may we forever have the courage to share the stories our Father has gifted us, that we might encourage others to run to Him and experience the miracles of God written on their own hearts. He is the God of miracles, and He is the same God yesterday, as today, as tomorrow.

Leah J Riggenbach

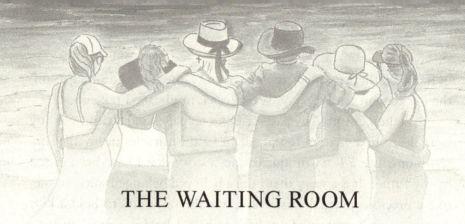

THE WAITING ROOM

"Be still, and know that I am God;"

PSALM 46:10 (NEW INTERNATIONAL VERSION)

The waiting room is a hard place to be. I have been in the waiting room. Have you? I waited to graduate from high school and then college. I waited to find the right husband and then waited for children. I waited for new job opportunities. And sometimes I waited for more unpleasant things when I had a difficult health diagnosis or watched someone I love leave this earth.

Are you in the waiting room? What are you waiting for? If you are, it's time to talk to the Lord and tell Him about your pain, sorrows, disappointments, and concerns. We often forget that God has a plan for our lives, and He knows our future. Jeremiah 29:11 says it all, "For I know the plans I have for you." When we talk to the Lord, asking for His wisdom to make the right decision, He may say yes—and how easy is that. Or He may say no which brings some disappointment or even discouragement, but at least there is an answer. But sometimes He makes us wait. For me, the waiting room is a difficult place to be.

When I consider the words of Psalm 46, "Know that I am God," I would tell you that I know Him. I grew up in a wonderful Christian home where I learned about God from parents, family, friends, and church. He is precious to me. I am aware of His presence, and I love to read His Word, talk to Him, and worship Him.

However, being "still" is something else! I'm not sure I can really

28

"be still." Yet, the Scripture tells us to "Be still and know…" I am trying harder to be still when waiting on the Lord. I know that no matter what happens, whether my life adventures have changed or ended, He knows me like no other. Dreams can die and doors can close, but He is alive and dwells within. So, I would say to you, learn along with me to be still and know that HE is GOD! Eventually, He will bring you out of the waiting room!

Judy Imperial

Viera, Florida Sign - Photo credit: Bernadette Skipper

DEFINING OUR IDENTITY

"Therefore, there is now no condemnation for those who are in Christ Jesus,"

ROMANS 8:1 (NEW INTERNATIONAL VERSION)

When someone asks the question "Who are you?", what do you say? I say I am a mother, grandmother, sister, daughter, friend, mentor, dog owner, and so on. Am I defined by my current life, my work, or my past? What defines me?

In college, I majored in Psychology and was intrigued by Erikson's theory of identity development. He taught that humans experienced 8 distinct stages from birth to adulthood. I won't bore you by going through each of the stages in detail, but I will say that much of our identity is shaped by our lived experiences – especially our those in our early years.

I grew up in the church – Sunday school, church service (I wasn't the best at sitting through service, but we didn't have a choice), Sunday night prayer service, Wednesday night CYC (the Wesleyan version of Awana), countless potlucks and other church gatherings – it was a prominent part of my life. Other than school, church was my place of social experiences, surrounded by a church family in which I knew I belonged. My understanding of right and wrong was drafted by a combination of Bible stories, songs, and scripture memorization, and I knew what was expected of me – but I never really got the "why" behind it.

I somehow got the feeling that appearances mattered most, and as long as everyone else saw me as a "perfect Christian" it was okay if inside I was far from it. I learned early-on how to fake it, and never show the truth. I don't remember ever hearing or understanding the meaning of "finding my identity in Christ", so I looked for it in the wrong places: friendships and relationships that were not centered in Christ. I remember attending camps and retreats and having a so-called "mountaintop experience", dedicating my life to God, but not really understanding what it meant or following up with it. Once I returned home, I was back to my old ways, and this cycle continued through my teen years up until I became a wife and mother and beyond. I was an imposter, and it seemed as though everyone knew it but me. The fact that others knew my life choices and mistakes kept me from ever really accepting God's forgiveness. I mean, no one would believe I could change – what would they say?

There is a chapter in the Purpose Driven Life, by Rick Warren, that asks the reader, "what defines you?" As I went through this study in 2003, I realized that I was struggling to move forward in my relationship with Christ because I was still focused on the sins of my past. I knew God loved me, but I did not truly believe He could or would forgive my sins – they were way too big. Of course, I was wrong, everything in my life – all of my sins and mistakes – had led me to the realization that I could not go on living in my old identity. In Christ was the only way to live. Romans chapter 8 contains so many of my favorite verses in scripture. The first verse of the chapter says, "there is now no condemnation for those who are in Christ Jesus." Verse 15 tells me I am no longer a slave to my old ways, but that I have been adopted by my heavenly father. If I am struggling to find the words to pray, verse 26 says that the Spirit will intercede for me. The chapter closes out by assuring me that "nothing can separate me from the love of God that is in Christ Jesus our Lord".

The old me was defined by the mistakes I made, or what others thought of me. Christ has changed me from the inside, and I now know what it feels like to live in Christ. I love the quote by Zig Ziglar that says, "Live in such a way that if someone spoke badly of you, no one would believe it." While I still care what people think or say about me, I am no longer defined by it. I want to live in such a way that if someone speaks badly of me, *I* won't believe it. I won't let it define my identity, because only my Father in Heaven can do that.

What defines you? Where do you find your identity? I believe it can only be found IN CHRIST.

Tracy Glidden

RESCUE

"I prayed to the LORD, and he answered me; he freed me from all my fears."

PSALM 34:4 (NEW LIVING TRANSLATION)

Rescue: verb - to save (someone) from a dangerous or distressing situation

noun - an act of saving or being saved from danger or distress

In the spring of 2021, I found myself drowning. I had been struggling in my marriage for over two decades. The intense fear of being alone led to the feeling of being chained to my current relationship. One evening, a friend began to press me about my marriage. Having survived a difficult marriage of her own, she shared her experience with me and urged me to end my failing marriage. I will never forget her words. Her support gave me the courage I needed to take this leap of faith.

Shortly afterwards, one Sunday morning I was watching television and I cried out to God, "Throw me a life preserver." I began switching TV stations and immediately found a station with a church service. The service offered me comfort and was the lifeline from God that I needed. I grabbed hold and hung on tightly. I had been raised in a devout Christian family but life's distractions had led me to set God aside. I had abandoned attending church and I had neglected honoring God, never giving Him the time He so deserved. But, when I asked for His help, He gave it unconditionally.

In the fall of 2021, I again asked for God's help, and through another friend, I was led to a women's Bible study at a local church. I remember my first day there was quite emotional. I was in tears most of the day upon realizing that all of these Christian women truly cared about Me! Their support carried me through the difficult months that followed until my divorce was final.

By the winter of 2021, I realized that I had made it! God had provided for me. He had washed away my fear and provided faith, strength, and courage. He had enabled me to navigate life on my own. He had blessed me with the friendships of other Christians who allowed me to lean on them when I needed. I knew I had not accomplished any of this alone.

I continued to build my relationship with God and as the calendar turned to 2022, I did what my father had asked me to do before he passed away—I began reading the Holy Bible. I have never enjoyed reading but now I can't get enough of God's Word. And God continues to give. Through a dear friend, I have met a wonderful man, my soulmate, who worships the Lord as I do. We are committed to learning more about our faith together. Each of us has suffered broken marriages and have prayed for genuine love. We recognize this miracle and sometimes question why we have been chosen to receive more than our share of blessings.

Now I want to share my experience of how God rescued me with unconditional love and strength! He has always been a constant in my life, even though at times I did not honor Him. But, I have come home. Always remember it is never too late. God waits with open arms; all we have to do is ask. I hope your journey will inspire others to follow His path and find courage in times of adversity.

Eleonora Christilles

PERMANENT RESIDENT

"The Lord is my strength and my song"

Psalm 118:14a (New Living Translation)

To be resilient, you must be strong with the Lord. That is a life lesson I know well and believe in unequivocally. Fortitude is a gift from the Holy Spirit which has enabled me to find the Lord and bring you this testament of faith in Him.

If anyone would have told me that the Lord was going to take permanent residence in my heart and stay there forever…there would have been a big fat, "Yeah right!"

I was raised in a staunchly religious home. In my youth, I resided with my grandmother in Spain, a country well known for their unfaltering Catholic faith, and those beliefs are continually drilled into every child's mind. I was at church every Sunday with my grandma because you needed a very good excuse for your absence or parents would not allow you to play with their children.

The rigidity of the dogma was so distasteful that I renounced the Catholic faith altogether. I didn't go to church for more years than I can count and the only prayers I uttered were the "save my keister prayers" when something truly went awry.

You may wonder what Facebook has to do with my story. Facebook may not be the most glamorous of social media platforms, but it has a way of reuniting friends you lost touch with long ago for some unfathomable reason. When I reconnected with one of my best friends, Tina, it was like that song, "Reunited and it feels so good."

We lived on opposite coasts, and although I did not know it at the time, she was going to be very instrumental in my being born again and embracing the Lord into my life.

In my opinion, I was not that much of a "goner"—I didn't do drugs or abuse alcohol, I wasn't promiscuous, I worked hard, and I helped others. On the outside I was always happy and, on the inside, I was never depressed, but I felt my life was quite meaningless and hollow. I had this cavernous emptiness in my soul that was constantly gnawing at me. I always felt very lonely and unfulfilled, so I buried myself in the brutal pace of my work.

I had a great life (I did, didn't I?) but it lacked solidity. I had been tainted by the lameness of quotidian life, where acquiring heaps of possessions, having shallow, rich friends, living in a killer house, and driving a swanky car was all there was to life. I know now that possessions will never truly define a person. I wanted to embrace the Christian faith, but I did not know how to.

All that began to change three years ago when I had a "come to Jesus" moment—that fork in the proverbial dusty road with a left and a right, where you have had enough and realize the time has come to reach out to the Lord to take your hand. Because I was struggling, feeling incredibly adrift, unhappy, unfulfilled, and vastly empty, my friend Tina put me in touch with a prayer warrior. From that time on, I began praying and talking to the Lord every day. He became my best friend. So now, everything was phenomenal. Then, I was diagnosed with stage IV cancer.

I crawled into a hole plagued with the habitual "why me?" question. Everyone walked around without a care in the world, and I wanted to be them—healthy and whole. For a month after my diagnosis, I lay in bed with that "who on earth cares," attitude. I went to treatment with the same attitude. Then I had that final "come to Jesus" moment—that broad fork in the dusty country road with no soul in sight—just me and God. I decided then and there to truly take His hand. That was the first day of the rest of my life.

Up to that moment, I had failed to realize that the Lord had been residing in my heart all along, patiently waiting, but it took a monumental, almost cataclysmic, event for me to truly sense His presence and truly believe in Him. He had sheltered me in so many ways and saved me so many times, unbeknownst to me at the time. I realized that during this incredibly arduous battle I'm fighting—it's not over—I know, like I know there's a dawn tomorrow, that He has healed me! Now I don't worry about anything because He has become my song, my hope, and my joy!

My work here isn't done. My story must be told through my writing and speaking, I want to inspire women everywhere to believe in Him wholeheartedly, no matter how many obstacles are along the road.

Miracles abound. They happen every day. There are angels that walk amongst us—have no doubt they do—guiding us and placing almost imperceptible signs that the Lord is speaking to us. We can't make sense of many things in life, but we must trust Him, as He always has a master plan.

Nanette Hebdige

FOCUSING ON WHAT COUNTS

"Be still and know that I am God"

PSALM 46:10A (NEW INTERNATIONAL VERSION)

"Be still and know that I am God" is one of my favorite Bible verses. Since I am a talker and a doer, being still requires serious conscious effort. It is especially difficult at bedtime to quiet that busy voice in my head. Since counting sheep has never helped, I decided to come up with my own counting system.

When I turned sixty-six, I memorized the sixty-six books of the Bible. On restless nights, I would recite the books in order and usually fall asleep before I reached Revelation. For a while, that helped me "be still" and fall asleep. But, as time passed, I could swiftly name all sixty-six books and still be wide awake.

I needed a new plan. So next, I memorized a verse which eloquently expresses the gospel of Jesus Christ in John 3:16, and then verses in Ephesians 6 reminding us of the armor that protects us from the devil. As before, in time, I was able to recite those verses and still be wide awake. As this process played itself out, I mastered more and more passages from the Word of God.

Romans 12:2, tells us to "be transformed by the renewal of your mind." My counting and memorizing system have helped me to renew my mind and enabled me to refocus on thoughts that have value. When I recite the Word of God, a renewed peace permeates my whole being.

Here are a few other amazing sections of the Bible that are certainly worth memorizing:

> The fruits of the Spirit listed in the book of Galatians
> The Ten Commandments recorded in the book of Exodus
> Jesus' "I Am" statements written in the gospels
> The names of Godly men and women recorded in the "Hall of Faith"
> Names of the women in the Scriptures

Lynn Edwards

HE WILL NEVER LEAVE YOU

"The LORD himself goes before you and will be with you;
He will never leave you nor forsake you."

DEUTERONOMY 31:8 (NEW INTERNATIONAL VERSION)

I was born into an extensive and loving Roman Catholic Italian family. I am the oldest of seventeen grandchildren on my mother's side, making me a princess and a happy spoiled kid. I was in church every Sunday from the earliest time I could remember, and I made my first holy communion at age seven. I knew God was that person I saw upon the cross and that He was in heaven, but I was not sure what heaven was or where it was. I followed religious teaching because that's what you did when mom and dad told you what to do.

At this time, the person I was madly in love with was my "daddy." Yes, I loved my mom and the entire family, but I was daddy's girl. I have great memories of him picking me up at school in his vast 18-wheeler truck. Life was beautiful until at eight years old my world crashed around me. I will never forget when I found my father across my bed, clutching his chest and his face etched in pain. I screamed for my mom who came running upstairs, and the next thing I knew, my father was being loaded into an ambulance. The last thing he ever said to me was, "I love you, Maria. You take care of your mom and sister." I never saw my dad alive again. He was just thirty-three years old when he left us—I was eight years old. I was left with my mom and my newborn baby sister.

I was devastated and despondent. Though my entire family of aunts, uncles, grandparents, and cousins surrounded me, I did not want to see one of them. I wanted my daddy. The family decided that perhaps a priest could help, so one day a priest was at the house telling me that God took my father to heaven, but He left me my sister. Those were not the words I wanted to hear. I told the priest to tell God to give my father back and to take my sister. After all, she was only a month old so she couldn't do anything with me.

That's when I began my journey of knowing there was a God, but I didn't like Him. Of course, I had to obey my family and go to church every Sunday, look up at the cross, and be mad every Sunday. As time went on, I always had God in my life, but I never really paid attention to Him.

Life went on. I learned to live without my dad. I grew up and became successful in my job in the airline industry and after that, even more successful in the corporate world. Yes, I still went to church and did all the ceremonial things I was supposed to. I got married and divorced within two years and then went into what I call "going into the wilderness." Looking back at that time in my life and the things I did, I can only believe someone was watching over me. Some of my wilderness days were wild and could have been harmful. Many years later, I was remarried to someone who believed in God but only called on God when He was needed. We were together for sixteen years, and then I went through another divorce.

Yes, I still went to church, and yes, I still kept God at a distance. But God had given me a very faithful grandmother who said her rosary every morning and sat in her chair by the window to read her Bible in Italian, which was rare in the faith I was raised. She was always one of my biggest supporters, and I loved her dearly. In Italian, she would always say," God bless you, Maria, God is watching over you, and it will be okay." She was so right.

After my second divorce, I was devastated. I got down on my knees and prayed alone in my big house, asking God what I was to do. As only God can do, He led me to a group called DivorceCare, and that is where I met HIM. DivorceCare helped support me through my divorce, it brought Christian women into my life, and it led me back to God.

As I look back on my life, I truly believe someone had to be watching over me. I had always wanted it to be my dad, but I now know it was God. Though there is more to my life story, the vital reality I have learned is that God never leaves you. He is always watching over you, even when you are walking away from Him. He always leads you to the life plan HE has for you. There are times we don't understand the why and we may never know His reasons. We don't need to know the why because we know HE is always with us.

Oh, just to let you know, I fell madly in love with my baby sister, and I am so glad God didn't take her back!

Maria Santa

WHO IS DRIVING YOUR THOUGHTS?

"My thoughts are nothing like your thoughts,' says the LORD.
'And my ways are far beyond anything you could imagine.
For just as the heavens are higher than the earth,
so my ways are higher than your ways
and my thoughts higher than your thoughts.'"

ISAIAH 55:8-9 (NEW LIVING TRANSLATION)

Have you ever noticed the number of thoughts that flood your mind while driving alone? Perhaps the thoughts could be planning your next conversation with the person you are going to visit or running your grocery list through your head or reminiscing over a memory when a certain song plays on the radio. What about the thoughts that build up anxiety? Maybe you are thinking of every worst-case scenario that could happen in a day. The "what-if's" may flood your brain as you are headed to the doctor. My personal challenge is the replay button that keeps running every WRONG thing I said to my teenager after she made a poor decision. What do we do when THOSE thoughts invade our mind?

Some dear friends gave me the best advice for when my mind and heart are being overtaken by negative thoughts. Once I realize where my mind is headed, I say out loud (I Kings 8:39 tells us only God can read our mind) "Satan, get out of my car!" As most of you know, the enemy comes to "steal and kill and destroy." (John 10:10). He is literally bringing his "Hell" to our thoughts. Our minds are very powerful and can dictate both our choices and our actions. Why wouldn't the enemy try to use that against us?

Think about a situation I'm sure we've all experienced (in some form or fashion)—you are running late because your child had a meltdown. First, you are stuck in traffic. Then, you have gotten cutoff by another car. Now, your gas tank gauge is on empty. What kind of thoughts are running through your head? Here it comes, "Satan, get out of my car. You are NOT allowed here. In the name of Jesus, leave NOW. Father God, I know I can't take on the day by myself. Jesus, take the wheel and protect me and guard my thoughts." It may not always feel like you won the battle, but this is a step in the right direction. Let go and let God.

"For the LORD your God is going with you! He will fight for you against your enemies, and he will give you victory!"

DEUTERONOMY 20:4 NLT

Christine Abad

Boardwalk - Photo credit: Bernadette Skipper

REST FOR THE WEARY

"Come to me, all of you who are weary and burdened, and I will give you rest."

MATTHEW 11:28 (NEW INTERNATIONAL VERSION)

In 1988, my husband and I bought a cottage on Butterfield Lake in upstate New York. With that gift from God, I promised I would share our cottage with others so they too could experience the lake and the wildlife which made their home there.

Little did I know that our cottage would become a haven for so many weary folks. We ran the cottage as though it were a Bed and Breakfast. We hosted pastors and their wives, burdened folks recovering from placing loved ones in nursing homes, executives looking for relaxation, and families with children wanting a day of fun near the water. Until we turned our cottage over to our children, I kept a journal of our visitors and I recorded stories about life at the lake with our visitors.

The lake is small but beautiful. It hosts loons, ospreys, egrets and great fishing for walleyes, bass, northern pike, and panfish. We have stories in which fishing poles, anchors and minnow buckets were lost in the lake, all to the amusement of the guests.

One story will always stand out from the rest. For many years, on Sundays our children were taught Bible stories by a wonderful couple in a nearby church. In later years, the wife had to be placed in a long term care facility. Around that time, the husband asked if he might visit us at the cottage. Of course, we said yes and I prepared food for his arrival. However, through a mix-up, he did not come on the appointed date. Our visitor finally showed up a couple days later. After rearranging our schedule, I tried to be gracious despite the inconvenience and we invited him to stay overnight. My husband and I realized that this tired, lonely visitor's heart was broken and in need of comforting. The next day was Sunday and we invited him to join us at our church. Our pastor gave a sermon that day about painful decisions that we have to make. As the sermon progressed, I looked over at our visitor and saw that he was sobbing. Later, he confided in us that the sermon was meant for him, and he now could better understand that God had led him in placing his wife in a home.

My husband and I have been blessed from even the heartaches that our guests have shared with us. Many of our guest's goodbyes ended with, "We really needed this break and thank you for inviting us to share this beautiful lake." We are grateful that God has used our cottage as a refuge for the weary and the burdened.

Beverly Cliffe

HOPE FOR THE FUTURE

"For I know the plans I have for you," declares the LORD, "plans to prosper you
and not to harm you, plans to give you hope and a future."

JEREMIAH 29:11 (NEW INTERNATIONAL VERSION)

Some years ago, I broke my right leg just below the knee. I had gotten my foot stuck on the corner of my desk at work and I fell down hard. I was in a cast from my hip down to my toes for several weeks and afterwards started physical therapy. During therapy I could not bend my knee when trying to exercise on the stationary bike. I was quite perturbed when the therapist accused me that I wasn't trying hard enough. I went back to see my doctor. He examined my leg and said there was scar tissue built up in my knee and he needed to do a manipulation while under anesthesia to get my joint moving. I went back to work and told my boss that I would hold off on the procedure until our quarter ended. Being a committed employee, I had only missed one day of work and wanted to see the company through the end of the quarter. Since I could not drive, someone had to bring me to and from work every day.

The day after the quarter ended, just before I was to have the procedure, the company laid me off. I was in shock. I had worked hard for this company; I took work home with me, worked countless weekends putting work before my kids and had even put my own health on hold for the company. I wondered how I was going to survive, pay my bills and take care of my two middle school girls. Because I was a single mother and I had recently purchased a condominium, I was in a dire situation. I decided I would look for another job after the medical procedure.

I went ahead with the procedure, but it didn't go as planned. There was a complication and the bone above my knee broke. I was back in another long cast and in terrible pain. I changed doctors and the new one said I needed surgery to clean out the scar tissue. After surgery, I was placed in a machine to keep my knee regularly moving so scar tissue would not form again. I was strapped in the machine all day and all night. I felt trapped and I became depressed. I mulled over all the negatives in my life—job loss, pain, recurrent surgery, and my incapacity. I kept thinking about everything I had ever done wrong!

One day I got a call from my older sister who was checking up on me. I told her I did not understand why these awful things were happening to me. She said that sometimes God allows unfortunate things to happen in our lives for our own good. She explained that when a refiner puts precious metal in a fire, the impurities in the metal boil to the top leaving only the best and purest of the metal. In the same way, God may allow us to go through the fire of difficulty to cleanse us of the impurities we need to be rid of in our lives. My sister helped me realize that I needed to change my life and start living according to what is pleasing to God.

As I determined to follow her advice, I was thankfully able to get rides to church and Bible studies. One Bible verse that stood out was Jeremiah 29:11, "For I know the plans I have for you," declares the LORD, "plans to prosper you and not to harm you, plans to give you hope and a future." I held onto that verse as God's promise to me that He doesn't want to harm me, and He has a plan for my future.

I needed several more surgeries, but I realized that God allowed those circumstances in my life to get my attention so that I would turn away from the life of sin I was living. Though it was a relentlessly difficult experience, I am grateful to God that those circumstances took place to change my life so I could worship and praise Him. God is faithful and His promise for a future has encompassed many things in my life. He even allowed me to meet my husband at church!

Terri O'Callaghan

MORE THAN YOU CAN IMAGINE

"Now to him who is able to do immeasurably more than all we ask or imagine, according to his power that is at work within us, to him be the glory in the church and in Christ Jesus throughout all generations, for ever and ever! Amen."

EPHESIANS 3:20-21 (NEW INTERNATIONAL VERSION)

Twenty years ago, I gave birth to my second son and one month later we packed the family, truck, belongings, dogs and all, and headed 1300 miles south to start a new life in Florida. Paradise wasn't quite what I had hoped for that first year. I was terribly depressed. I had left a career, family, friends, and all that I had ever known. We moved to an area where we did not have anyone that we knew close by. By close by, I mean within stroller walking distance. No babysitters, no relatives, no one. I am not even much of a "people person," but I was lonely. We were struggling to set a foundation. I was not working. It was hard getting used to new places and things, and we didn't have a church...yet.

During all of that, I always had my faith and I have always known that God was for me. We went through ups and downs that first year. We finally moved from the middle of nowhere...for real, nowhere. There were rattlesnakes and boars in that yard! I grew up in the city. We moved to the Viera area. Once we were settled, we went church shopping. Again, something I don't care for...shopping! But, we found and felt comfortable at Church At Viera (CAV). I was praying that now my husband and I could create the life we always talked about. Boy, did God know what He was doing there! My children were instantly loved on and loved being at CAV. Slowly but surely, we both became involved in CAV in some way. We were baptized together in 2005. During the first two years at CAV, we volunteered in the toddler nursery. Each of us also spent time in men's and women's ministries. Our marriage was hard, I mean HARD. Through it all, till the very end, I prayed. I prayed for my husband. I imagined us building a business as a legacy for our children. I prayed about our family members. I imagined that our children would all grow to love the Lord and each other. I prayed for healing. I imagined a time of peace. I prayed for our finances. I prayed and asked God to come through.

Some of those things I anticipate still, but some of those things have been experienced immeasurably more than I could have imagined! The business is growing, several of the children are becoming adults who know Jesus, and they all love each other. There was a relationship healing, there were finances that came through in the nick of time, and there have been times of peace, even after losing my husband. The deepest peace is in knowing that Jesus is my Savior and that He can do so much with His power that is at work within us.

Carole Hoover

MORE OF HIM AND LESS OF ME

"He must increase, but I must decrease."

JOHN 3:30 (NEW KING JAMES VERSION)

I magine having worked diligently on a big project—one that took a lot of your time, energy and creativity. You were feeling accomplished and excited to share the end results of your hard work. Then someone else comes along who takes most of the credit for your work. What would you do? The mind games begin in your head.

Remember that our purpose here certainly is not to make ourselves look good. It is to make much of Jesus in this world through the way we live our lives! It is to give Him the Glory because, if you think about it, you could never have started that big project without Jesus!

I love the way John the Baptist humbly acknowledges and is honored by being a part of God's plan. He worked to lift Jesus up in front of the multitudes. John speaks of a faithful follower being "the friend to the bridegroom" and "rejoicing greatly" upon hearing the bridegroom's voice, and saying, "this joy of mine is fulfilled."

Who wants to have a friend like John the Baptist? Someone who is so assured in Christ that they are ok with the spotlight on Jesus and not themselves. They joyfully and freely give Him the glory and honor always. "He must increase, but I must decrease," (John 3:30).

Decreasing is hard when thinking in a worldly way. We tend to want things like a new job, more money, bigger house, newer this or that. We even sometimes are willing to sacrifice, save up for a while, for the next best thing. If we start from this verse in John, if we start by thinking about decreasing oneself so that we can increase God in our lives, what then? Watch as He flourishes in your heart for His Glory!

Stated simply, read and soak up God's word. Embed it in your heart. Yearn for and learn from God and let God use you. Lean on Him for your understanding and bring Him glory.

Shonna Cottrell

POWER THROUGH HIM

"His divine power has granted to us all things that pertain to life and godliness, through the knowledge of him who called us."

II Peter 1:3 (English Standard Version)

T he Word of God is full of what "life" should look like. Many live their life trying to please other people, or live in self-reliance with minimal thought of others. Both can be a trap for the enemy to use. When we focus on pleasing others, we neglect our focus on our Savior. When we do not have regard for others, then we become self-centered. God's word says in Philippians 2:3 ESV, "Do nothing from selfish ambition or conceit, but in humility count others more significant than yourselves." Love one another.

Godliness comes through living out His Word as it is described in I Thessalonians 5:14- 18, "Be patient with them all. See that no one repays anyone evil for evil, but always seek to do good to one another and to everyone. Rejoice always, pray without ceasing, give thanks in all circumstances." We cannot do this in our own strength. In Ephesians 6:10, God calls us to be strong in the Lord and in the power of HIS might. The only way to navigate this life is through His power, gaining knowledge of Him through the Scriptures.

The first part of my life was full of selfishness because I was struggling to survive in my own flesh due to circumstances. I did not even notice others, but God saw me and called me by name! Unfortunately, when I became a Christ follower, I often looked to other people to define myself. I saw other's approval as more important than the Lord's. I followed all the rules, I went to church every time the doors were open, but it never seemed to be good enough. Once I placed my identity in Christ, there was freedom! I now sought to please God and live in His unconditional love for and acceptance of me. My relationship with God and others flourished. I didn't just read Scripture, I experienced it. I chose humility, gentleness, love, and peace as Ephesians 4 directs us to do. I chose to let go of bitterness, anger, and evil speaking. I daily chose to be kind, tenderhearted, and forgiving because God in Christ enables me to do so! My life verse has always been Ephesians 3:20-21 ESV, "Now to him who is able to do far more abundantly than all that we ask or think, according to the power at work within us, to him be the glory." Now, I cherish God's Word—I want my life to mirror Nehemiah 8:10 which says, "The joy of the Lord is my strength."

Karen Sheldon

CONTRADICTORY

"For what shall it profit a man, if he shall gain the whole world, and lose his own soul?"

MARK 8:36 (KING JAMES VERSION)

I thought my season of loss was over. I thought I was done losing things, but now I'm losing everything. My home, my furniture, my clothes, my independence, slowly slipping from my grip.

I endured a disheartening season of loss a few years earlier. It began with the unanticipated death of my sweet friend…then my great grandmother…then my caring brother. Three major deaths within 366 days. By the spring of 2019, my whole world had fallen apart. I was twenty-one years old.

I thought that season had ended, but here I am now, twenty-four and losing everything once more. At least, it feels as though I am losing everything.

While I sit here lamenting my losses, the faintest echo creeps into my mind—what does it profit a man to gain the whole world and lose his soul? I lost people in 2019, and now I am losing possessions. I cry out, "God, how much more will you take?" I recall His promises— "The LORD God is a sun and a shield: the LORD will give grace and glory: no good thing does he withhold from them that walk uprightly," Psalm 84:11 KJV.

It's tempting to dwindle life down to losses, but I have watched too many people lose their souls to the idleness of the world. Loss plagues us in this world so full of sorrows, but perhaps these losses awaken the ache in our souls for something more. Loss chisels its way through the busyness, through the plans, through the dreams. Loss unearths our frailty. So tempted to break, and yet so contradictorily strong.

We lose our souls when we hold onto the hope of people and possessions. We should mourn our losses and thank God for the sorrow—our beautiful hearts longing for things as they should be, as God intended them to be when He created the universe—and in our losses, we must remember what we gain. While we cannot see the victories through our pain, a hidden beauty runs through our veins.

God employs these compounding losses to save our throbbing souls.

Hope A. Charters

Artemis rollout Kennedy Space Center - Photo credit: Linda Foster

GOD LOVES TO RECYCLE

"He comforts us in all our troubles so that we can comfort others.
When they are troubled, we will be able to give them the same comfort
God has given us."

II CORINTHIANS 1:4 (NEW LIVING TRANSLATION)

The rate at which humanity wastes and discards limited resources has grown tremendously in recent decades. In our hurried lives we crave disposable items as we move through life "on the go" at an increased pace. Passionate voices behind the recycle and reuse movements have presented catchy campaigns, hard data, and persuasive reasons for us to reuse, recycle, and repurpose. Amidst a culture and society so focused on reusing tangible resources, we must not miss the brilliance in the fact that the Giver and Creator of all resources, has demonstrated a model of recycling from the beginning of time.

Truly, God is in the recycling business. All throughout the Bible we see God repurpose and reuse lives who have unbelievable amounts of garbage in them. Noah was a drunk, David was an adulterer, Jonah ran from God in rebellion, Paul was a murderer—the list goes on and on through our Bible genealogy of heroes of the faith. Our faith in Jesus offers us so much more than forgiveness of sins and eternity in heaven. God's offer to every believer is new life here on earth, an exchange of the trash of your past for a repurposed future.

Every one of us has baggage. We've hurt others. Others have hurt us. We've lived selfishly. We've been angry, hateful, jealous, bitter, prideful, lustful and impatient. We've all done things we are ashamed of, and it's easy to cringe at the thought of the garbage that is unique to our "life trash can" being pulled out to be recycled. The enemy of our souls so easily tricks Christians into living in such a viscous shame cycle that we beg Jesus to just take our trash away!

"Dispose of it quietly…" we plead.

Romans 8:28 (NIV) says, "In all things God works for the good of those who love him, who have been called according to his purpose."

God has a purpose and a redemptive plan, even in our failures. I believe that one of the ways this purpose plays out most practically in our lives is when we cooperate with the way God desires to recycle our regrets, mistakes, and suffering. Sadly, our world has prevalent suffering, trials, unexpected hardships, and unfair circumstances that consistently weave in and out of each of our lives on an almost daily basis. None of us are exempt, and though we grapple and strive for control or predictability of our future, it can never be adequately attained.

2 Corinthians 1:4 lays out God's recycling plan for our lives with such a purpose—"He comforts us in all our troubles so that we can comfort others. When they are troubled, we will be able to give them the same comfort God has given us."

God guides us, strengthens us, enables us, protects us, and moves us through "life's moments" so that we can recycle our experiences of His faithfulness to help others. As God recycles our lives, He uses our testimonies to provide tangible references to the promises found in Scripture. When we've experienced joy in the middle of heartbreaking circumstances, we exemplify hope in the darkness, (Ps 30:11). When we've experienced provision in dire circumstances, we can testify to the God who controls all the riches in the world, (Matthew 6:31-32). When we've experienced His protection against those who slander or who wish to harm us, we are living proof that even when others mean harm, God can shield, undo, or thwart their advances, (Genesis 50:20).

Just as one must be intentional about recycling physically here on earth, we must be equally diligent in allowing God to recycle our life garbage. We must cooperate in allowing Him to take our trash, expose it, break it down, remanufacture and repurpose it however He sees fit. We must be receptive and responsive to the still and quiet voice that leads us in this process. I truly believe God desires to waste nothing in our lives. Every experience, hardship and trial can be used to refine us, encourage others, and give Him glory.

Friends, every day you are given a choice. You can choose to wastefully trash your life experiences, or you can be intentional about inviting God to recycle your trash and bring forth treasure.

Christina Stolaas

THE SOVEREIGNTY OF GOD

"The LORD will fulfill His purpose for me. LORD, your faithful love endures forever."

It was an exquisite day as my husband and I drove from San Antonio, Texas, to Hampton, Virginia. Although it was a long drive, we were both looking forward to the in-depth talks we always enjoyed on our long car rides together. The smell of coffee wafted in our car as we discussed how excited we were to hug our grown children and snuggle with our grandchildren once we arrived in Virginia. We shared personal struggles as well as victories in Christ. There were several years to look back on and see the mighty hand of God and where He has brought us today. Recently, our pastor had shared that the second half of life is when you learn to "play with injuries." We discussed the "injuries" life had thrown our way and the faithfulness of God who helped us to make it through those difficult times.

All of a the sudden, the strangest phenomenon occurred. We were driving over a tall bridge when I noticed that on the left side of the bridge it was beautifully sunny and calm. The sunrise was absolutely breathtaking and surreal. On the right side of the bridge there were dark and luminous clouds. It looked like a storm was brewing. The Lord spoke softly to my heart. He told me that as I traveled a long road to Virginia, I had the choice to fix my eyes on all the beauty along the way, or to dwell on the dark and stormy happenings around

64

me. Either way, I was still going to Virginia. So it is with my life, I have the choice to gaze upon the beauty and joy of life, or dwell on the darkness and evil in this world. Either way, because I am a daughter of the Most High King, my destination is the same, in heaven with God for eternity.

What about you? Where will you focus your gaze? Will you rest in God's faithful love and trust Him as He fulfills His purpose for you? Or will you focus on the world around you and drown in turmoil and anxiety? If you have given your life to Jesus and trusted Him as your Lord and Savior, heaven is your eternal home!

If you have not given your life to Jesus, you can right now! God gave us clear instructions in the Bible so you can know heaven will be your home: "If you confess with your mouth, 'Jesus is Lord,' and believe in your heart that God raised him from the dead, you will be saved. One believes with the heart, resulting in righteousness, and one confesses with the mouth, resulting in salvation," Romans 10:9–10 CSB.

God loves you more than you can possibly imagine. His plans for you are glorious! Will you ask Jesus to forgive you of your sins and acknowledge your need for Him as Lord of your life today? No longer do you have to face difficulties on your own. God tells us to, "Cast your burden on the Lord, and he will sustain you; he will never allow the righteous to be shaken," Psalm 55:22 CSB. Right now, you can give your burdens to God and allow Him to handle them. "He himself has said, I will never leave you or abandon you," Hebrews 13:5 CSB. You are not alone; God will always be with you. Although life is full of suffering and trials, it is also full of joy and blessings. Let's choose today to focus our gaze on all the beauty and joy which God created for us in this journey called life!

Harmony Charters

THE GREATEST GIFT IS LOVE

"And now these three remain: faith, hope and love. But the greatest of these is love."

I CORINTHIANS 13:13 (NEW INTERNATIONAL VERSION)

This Scripture on love is often used at weddings, including my own almost twenty-eight years ago. The meaning behind this Scripture isn't focused on romantic love. The verse is not simply a standard for what love in a marriage should look like. This passage extends way beyond the bonds of matrimony. I Corinthians shares in detail what a Christ-like love does and does not do. As I considered this Scripture, I realized I had not even begun to fully explore the depths of genuine love.

Fast forward to 2019—my mom died from lung cancer. She fought the disease for a year and a half with me by her side as her medical advocate. I was her oldest of her five children. After her passing, I imagined my siblings and me drawing closer together during a common bond of grief. To my dismay, her death seemed to fracture our relationships instead of strengthening those. It created a chasm of anger, hurt, and resentment between us five. At that time, I was dumbfounded at our various displays of negative emotions in the midst of our shared sorrow. Two of my three brothers refused to even talk with me. I was cut off even as I pleaded to get together and discuss our pain. At the start of this lack of communication, I placed the blame upon their shoulders and went through a kaleidoscope of negative emotions for months. I felt I had done nothing wrong, yet this situation wasn't right. Somehow the Lord broke through that tough wall I had constructed in my heavy heart. He led me to study the love chapter. I went deep—I wrote every word out on paper. What was I doing wrong and what, if any, was I doing right? I asked God to open my heart to His wisdom, truth, and guidance. So, what happens when you fervently pray? Oh my! In His profoundly, quiet way He showed me uncomfortable truths about myself.

"Love is patient, love is kind. It does not envy, it does not boast, it is not proud. It does not dishonor others, it is not self-seeking, it is not easily angered, it keeps no record of wrongs. Love does not delight in evil but rejoices with the truth. It always protects, always trusts, always hopes, always perseveres. Love never fails," I Corinthians 13:4-8 NIV.

"And now these three remain: faith, hope, and love. But the greatest of these is love,"
I Corinthians 13:13 NIV.

I dissected every word. Love is patient. Am I patient? More specifically, am I patient with my brothers? I answered yes. Love is kind. Am I kind to my brothers? Yes, of course I am. I continued throughout every word. I answered every single question honestly. It was soul-wrenching and painful in spots. Through the help of the Holy Spirit, I discovered that my biggest failure about love was that I often dwelled on the past hurts that my brothers caused me.

I was constantly thinking about all the moments that caused me anger, hurt, and disappointments—certainly nothing excellent or praiseworthy, the concepts that we were encouraged to dwell on in Philippians 4:8! I was guilty of holding a record of wrongs! Once I had the realization that I wasn't truly forgiving of certain painful moments from the past, it also brought to light that I wasn't fulfilling the other components to love either. I couldn't be completely patient or kind if I am harboring bad thoughts about a person.

What about the other aspects of love—protects, trusts, hopes, and perseveres? Nope! Not when I was eager to heap blame on my brothers' shoulders. Okay, Lord, what do I do now with these tough truths about myself? I continued to pray, be still, and wait for God's guidance.

I waited for two months. In the span of just one week, not just one, but both brothers got in touch with me! I found myself filled with unconditional love for them both. I demonstrated love by actively listening to them. That was it! I can say that our relationships now have never been better. That is what God does—He turns brokenness into a beautiful restoration like only He can do. There is no doubt the Lord used this painful time in my life to teach and refine me. I will always be grateful to Him for this and so much more!

Dear Lord, thank you for teaching me about love. Romans 12:9 NIV begins with, "Love must be sincere." Holy Spirit, help me to love others sincerely and unconditionally. I pray to love at all times like Jesus! In His name I pray. Amen!

Stacey Sutton

THE GOD OF ALL COMFORT

"What a wonderful God we have. He is the Father of our Lord
Jesus Christ,
the source of every mercy, and the One who so wonderfully comforts
and strengthens us in our hardships and trials."

II CORINTHIANS 1:3 (THE LIVING BIBLE)

There are those defining moments in our lives that change the entire trajectory of the rest of our lives. That moment for me was the day after Thanksgiving in 1996. My husband and I were sitting in our living room and he very calmly looked at me and said," I have terminal cancer." In that moment, my heart was shattered and my soul was shredded. I was suddenly a bruised soul.

But this story is not about a seven year cancer battle. It is about the God of all comfort. In the ensuing days of that defining moment, I had to determine what I really believed about God. I had to determine that I could not let the assault of a terminal illness in my world become my identity. I could not change the reality of what life had become, but I could determine what my reaction would be. As A.W. Tozer wrote, "What I believe about God is the most important thing about me," and that statement had to be my anchor going forward. What did I believe about God?

I determined that I was not going to lose my joy of living. I was going to cling to Isaiah 43:1-3 (NASB), "Do not fear, for I have redeemed you; I have called you by name; and you are Mine! When you pass through the waters, I will be with you; And through the rivers, they will not overflow you. When you walk through the fire, you will not be scorched, nor will the flame burn you. For I am the Lord your God."

In what is sometimes called "the midnight hour," when fear and loneliness intrude, I recalled that God's gaze was always fixed on me and even when a storm raged around me, my heart and mind could be at rest. I could sleep, blanketed in peace, because God is bigger than anything I faced tomorrow.

My goal was not to know every detail of the future but to hold onto the hand of the One who does, and never let go. As I held His hand, these are the things I learned: some things in life cannot be fixed, they can only be carried; there isn't any valley HE is not in; my tearful prayers will always reach His ears; and I could not allow the grip of fear or the unknown creep in and take me where I did not want to go.

In Grief Share, we speak of "flash prayers." I had hundreds of those a day. In my devastating situation, it was often too difficult to articulate a prayer, but it brought me comfort to know that the Lord heard even my, "Oh God!" My heart was comforted by the wisdom of these often-repeated words: "When you cannot trace His hand, trust His heart."

My journey with Him through this process of total reliance began very tenuously but has become more assured and peaceful. Still, to this day, I desperately rest in God's grace and peace and in His promises. I still cry out to Him, but always with the absolute knowledge that He will never leave me or forsake me! God never abandons any of us, ever!

Many years ago, I heard a song entitled "Through it All." The first lines were: "Through it all I've learned to trust in God. Through it all I've learned to depend on His Word." I don't search for answers anymore. I have learned to live in a world where there are not many answers to our deepest questions, but God comforts us with the faith that He knows the answers.

Sue Lewis

DON'T WORRY…BE HAPPY!

"Do not be anxious about anything, but in every situation, by prayer and petition, with thanksgiving, present your requests to God. And the peace of God, which transcends all understanding, will guard your hearts and your minds in Christ Jesus."

PHILIPPIANS 4:6-7 (NEW INTERNATIONAL VERSION)

When I was first saved, I needed to know, meditate on, and fully believe this verse because my personality is inclined to be a worrier. I am the person who thinks "what could happen if…?" or, "What will I do if…?" and "How will I fix it?"

When I finally absorbed this verse, it was a game changer. Though it took me a while to learn not to attempt to control every situation, I finally realized that I can't, but Jesus certainly CAN. So now when I am stressed, I give my burdens, concerns, and fears to Him. The Bible has taught me that He will give me peace. It is truly amazing how "He guards my heart and mind."

God loves us so much that He takes care of even the smallest things.

Donna Ellis Etheridge

THE GOLDEN RULE

*"So in everything, do to others what you would have them
do to you, for this sums up the Law and the Prophets."*

MATTHEW 7:12 (NEW INTERNATIONAL VERSION)

My Dad loved to tell a story about something my cousin did when she was a child. He especially loved to tell this story when he and my cousin were in the same room. When my Dad started the story, my cousin lovingly rolled her eyes, and smiled fondly at my dad. She knew where this was going. Even though she had heard him tell the story on more than one occasion, and even though the story may not showcase her best childhood trait, she still enjoyed hearing him tell this story almost as much as he delighted in telling it. As the story goes, when my cousin was a child, about four or five- years-old, she went for a ride in the NEW family car with her Father. He made a stop at a local store and she waited in the car for him while he went inside. This was in the 1950's, so it was safe to do.

Apparently, while he was inside an "incident" occurred, which my cousin proudly reported to her father upon his return to the car. Did I mention this was a BRAND NEW car? My cousin said, "Daddy, while you were in the store, a man pulled up beside your car and when he opened his car door, he hit your brand new car with his door! So, you know what I did? I opened our car door and hit his car right back!"

Is this not a perfect example of "Do unto others as they do unto you?" The part of the story I don't recall hearing is if there was damage to either car.

What I do know is, even as Christians, we are sometimes tempted to behave like a five- year-old, treating others the same way in which they treat us. We fail to follow the scripture as we have been instructed by our heavenly Father, "Do to others as you would have them do to you"—treat others the way we would like to be treated— The Golden Rule. If we choose to treat others the way they treat us instead of the way we would like to be treated, unlike the car door story, the damage WILL be remembered by us, and also by others.

Kathy Peebles

Heart Shell Art - Photo credit: Bernadette Skipper

LIGHT OF THE WORLD

"The light shines in the darkness, and the darkness has not overcome it."

JOHN 1:5 (NEW INTERNATIONAL VERSION)

We have a light that is available to us if we choose to accept it. This light offers forgiveness. A light that erases shame and fear. A light that sees us and loves us through our darkest moments. This light is Jesus Christ.

Depression and anxiety have been with me most of my life. A darkness that seems to seep in between the cracks of my soul. The pain of this darkness made me want to give up on life. When I was a young teen, it led me to hurt myself. Cutting myself was a way to feel physical pain that would refocus the mental suffering for a moment. When I entered college, depression led me to physical addictions. Alcohol and sex were a way to numb the way I felt. Later in life, anxiety would cause me to not want to leave the house. Fear of anything different would stop me from attending social situations. Anxiety gripped me when I thought of all the "what-if's." I have gone to many therapists and have tried many remedies. Even though they have helped to a certain point, I was still struggling.

Only when I gave my life to Jesus, did I truly start to heal. Jesus' light was with me throughout all of this, and the darkness in me never overtook the light. Through prayer and reading God's Word I have strengthened my relationship with the Lord, and in turn He has shined His light on my mental struggles, blinding the darkness within me. It has been a long journey, with many ups and downs.

At one point in my walk with the Lord, I was so frustrated I ripped up a piece of paper and threw it on the ground and wept. When I went to pick up the pieces of paper, the torn letters now formed the words, "Enough, be still, I am." Here I was at such a low point, and the Lord beamed His light into my frustration, and reminded me who was in control. God is slowly maturing me and showing me what is important in life. When I keep my focus on Him and His healing light, I am able to move forward. In His strength, I am able to do more than I could ever imagine. I now am able to leave my house, attend Bible study, and even serve at the church. I am part of an incredible church community that has truly shown me what it means to love like Christ—all because of Him.

The Lord has brought me so far from where I was. I still struggle with depression and anxiety, but I have hope in my Lord and Savior. He has carried me this far and will continue to do so. One day I will go home to my Father and I will be made new, free from anxiety and depression. I know that no matter how dark it gets, that Jesus will never leave me. He too knows what it is like to suffer. He sympathizes with our afflictions. Whatever you are going through, whatever physical or mental pain, know that Jesus is there. You need only to ask. The darkness will never overcome the light of Jesus Christ.

Genevieve Peterson

THE CROSS ON THE TRUCK

"The rich rule over the poor, and the borrower is slave to the lender."

PROVERBS 22:7 (NEW INTERNATIONAL VERSION)

When I was single, working for a major company in Melbourne, Florida, I decided to buy a home and stop renting. I had a stable job. I was pre-approved for a loan, and I had a significant down payment. The amount for which I was approved seemed like a large number to me and I was excited! I looked at several homes and decided on a newer home near the top of my price range.

As I prayed on it, I asked God several questions. I asked if it was the right home, was I spending too much, should I really buy a home, and was it the right location? I started getting a feeling something wasn't right. I didn't know what the feeling was, so I prayed and prayed. I asked God to tell me straight up if I should move forward or if not, to open my eyes to understand what was not quite right.

I had to make a decision within a few days or lose the home I had my heart set on. I drove by the house many times just looking and dreaming of living there but something was nagging at me. I asked God for help or answers or a sign in a big way to let me know it was okay to move forward.

A couple of days later I was driving home from church and there was my answer! I was so excited. A pickup truck a few cars ahead of me had a huge wooden cross the size of the vehicle tied to the back of the tailgate. The cross was so big, I don't know how it stayed

77

in place, but it caught my attention. I thought, "Wow, God, you answered me!" The other cars turned off the road, so the truck was smack in front of me. I was jumping for joy until I read the Scripture on the cross. Proverbs 22:7 NIV: "The rich rule over the poor, and the borrower is slave to the lender."

I was hurt. I cried and was upset thinking "Why not? What did it mean? How could it mean I should not borrow the money?" But I knew in my heart it meant "No." I just didn't understand. My heart felt broken until a few short weeks later, when I was laid off with many others. It was nearly a year before I found another good paying position. My savings and support from close friends got me through. However, that did not compare to what God had done for me. He saved me from a financial disaster.

Valarie Campbell

CONNECTING THROUGH UNEXPECTED SCRIPTURES

"For the word of God is alive and active. Sharper than any double-edged sword, it penetrates even to dividing soul and spirit, joints and marrow;

it judges the thoughts and attitudes of the heart."

HEBREWS 4:12 (NEW INTERNATIONAL VERSION)

Let's be real here. The Bible can be intimidating, both to read and to talk about. This is the Word of God, right? Hebrews 4:12 says, "For the word of God is alive and active. Sharper than any double-edged sword, it penetrates even to dividing soul and spirit, joints and marrow; it judges the thoughts and attitudes of the heart." Had this been the first verse in the Bible I ever read, I don't think I would have continued. Fortunately for me, it was not.

I grew up reading a children's Bible. Most of my life, that seemed like enough. My children's Bible contained all the major themes and lessons that my "adult" Bible has but without those items that I mistakenly considered filler or unnoteworthy. Adult conversations I had about the Bible came with such heaviness and complexity that, as a busy mom with two kids already carrying a heavy load, I felt like I didn't need the extra weight. I love reading and when I do get a spare moment, I gravitate towards stories with surprising twists and shocking turns.

Then one day I was reading my "adult" Bible when I realized how WRONG I had been. I discovered there was so much value packed into the pages of my adult Bible that was missing from my children's Bible. I was unaware of the fascinating details and unexpected twists and turns in the lives of characters in the Bible. There are events in these stories that will leave you speechless and eager to tell someone: stories like Judges 4 (Jael did what?); and Matthew 27, a powerful story that moves you to tears; and Ezekiel 23 makes you blush and clutch your pearls. This book is both powerful and amazing! It can change your life.

That is exactly what happened to me. When I started reading these stories, the most beautiful thing happened. I started to have a real relationship with God. John 1:1 NIV says, "In the beginning was the Word, and the Word was with God, and the Word was God." By spending time in His word, I ultimately started to spend more time with Him. Each story I read had me asking more questions and led me to dive deeper into His Word for more knowledge.

At times, the Bible engages difficult subjects like incest, war, and sex. But Romans 1:16 says, "For I am not ashamed of the gospel, because it has the power of God that brings salvation to everyone who believes." There are so many colorful details that have left me speechless and now I find myself wanting to discuss them.

I chose a couple of friends and started talking. "Girl, did you hear about the man in the Book of Judges that cut off the thumbs and big toes of kings so they would become harmless warriors?" Often they chuckle because they weren't expecting my question. By sharing and discussing these stories, I have learned that God uses them for His purpose. The best part is getting to share the Word of God with someone else.

Connecting with someone through unexpected Scriptures can open a pathway for God to do what only God can do. So open your Bible, find the most unusual story you can, and go tell a friend about it. Watch how God works through these biblical anomalies.

Paige West

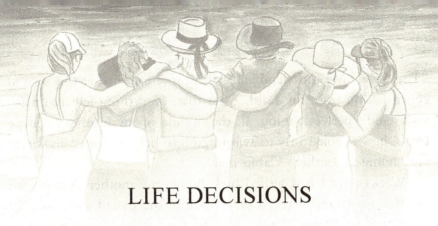

LIFE DECISIONS

"Trust in the LORD with all your heart"

PROVERBS 3:5A (THE OPEN BIBLE)

A s I left home at eighteen, leaving behind my two younger siblings and my mom who raised me in southern California, I moved to the state of Washington to get to know my dad and his wife. Then in my early twenties, I felt the Lord tugging at my heart for many weeks to move back near my mother again. I could not stop thinking about it, so daily I prayed deep heartfelt prayers asking God for guidance.

One night in February, as I read Psalms, I prayed and cried out for God to direct my steps. I didn't want to make a mistake, since I would be leaving a good job, friends at church and a nice boyfriend. I fell asleep praying the prayers of David in Psalm 119. Hours later, I was gently aroused by a bright light. I felt God telling me to go and trust Him. I was so filled by His presence of peace and joy as I thanked and praised the Lord for answering my prayer. I checked the time, and it was one in the morning—I had been asleep for several hours. I was so amazed that God heard and answered MY prayers and He even spoke to ME!

After the weekend of Valentines with Presidents Day off, I went to lunch with a friend from work and told her all about my experience. As we finished and paid the tab at the cash register, there was a bowl of Valentine Sweethearts candies with words printed on one side. I picked up one, flipped it over to see my word and it was,

"Trust Me." My girlfriend and I were so astonished at this second confirmation from the Lord. After that, everything fell into place with God's perfect timing. In the middle of my brother's college finals, he was able to fly to Washington to help me move and drive back home to southern California.

Weeks after I had settled back home, my mother shared with me that my grandmother's prayer before she passed away months earlier was that I would move back home. I am so very thankful for my grandmother Emma's prayers. This resulted in my mother and I becoming very close.

A couple of years later, while attending my local church one Sunday evening, I met my future husband, sitting right next to me. Now, after thirty-seven years of marriage and two daughters, I can see the Lord's hand in my life. So many blessings to be thankful for, including a new granddaughter. We are also very thankful for a wonderful church with true Bible-based teachings and sweet fellowship.

Lord Jesus, help us to nurture that small mustard seed of faith and to trust in You for ALL things. In Jesus' Name, Amen!

Psalm 55:16-17 The Living Bible "But I will call upon the Lord to save me—and He will. I will pray morning, noon, and night, pleading aloud with God; and he will hear and answer."

Psalm 119:31 TLB "I cling to your commands and follow them as closely as I can. Lord, don't let me make a mess of things."

Philippians 4: 6-7 TLB "Don't worry about anything; instead, pray about everything; tell God your needs, and don't forget to thank him for his answers. If you do this you will experience God's peace, which is far more wonderful than the human mind can understand. His peace will keep your thoughts and your hearts quiet and at rest as you trust in Christ Jesus."

Lori Braun

MEASURABLE SORROW

*"You keep track of all my sorrows.
You have collected my tears in your bottle.
You have recorded each one in your book."*

PSALM 56:8 (NEW LIVING TRANSLATION)

God can keep track of our sorrows because our sorrows are measurable. I remember being thirteen and imagining the colossal bottle God would need to store my tears. As I grew older, the image of the bottle faded from my mind. I became bitter and cynical, forgetting the God who cared enough to monitor my tossings and record my pain; replacing my conceptualization of God to someone else who had abandoned me.

Heyper-focusing on my unending emotional pain, I refused to believe that God cared for me. He couldn't—it just didn't make sense. I loved God desperately, but I had the most difficult time trusting Him.

When I was twenty-one, my brother took his life from me. He was a wonderfully duplicitous man, as most drug addicts are. He was kind and caring, but addiction consumed him and brought with it a host of uninviting traits.

The week before he died, I watched him pray earnestly in a hospital bed that God would help him overcome addiction, but God allowed my brother to take his life instead. That, that made no sense. I questioned everything. I reevaluated everything I had ever believed. I loved God, but I was beyond heartbroken, and I was too young to believe that God could bring goodness from something so horrifying.

Some run towards God in their sorrows. Others, like me, run away from Him. I ran, so terrified of reality and so afraid to trust Him. I fought to trust Him, but it seemed as though everything in life mocked me for trusting Him. The internal battle overwhelmed me—it was all so terrifying. I could barely pray.

God broke through my defensive walls five months after my brother's death, and I wrote:

"You love me. You loved me anyway. It is Your loving kindness that returns us to You. How great You are!

Lord, this is the hardest season I have ever endured. It's been so, so, so hard. You collect my tears in a ledger. You hold me when all I try to do is fall away from You, and You kindly, warmly, graciously welcome me back.

Everything is not okay. Everything is painful and everything is broken, but You bind my wounds. You heal me and You restore me.

I am alive! I am alive and therefore I have hope.

You never left me. You never let me go. You allowed me to break.

You came so that I may have life and have it to the full.

Your light shines in the darkness, and the darkness has not overcome it.

It's so dark.

But You are light, and You are near."

Overwhelming sorrow feels impossible to mitigate, irrational to define, and unfathomable to touch. Long-suffering consumes the griever with the dread that he or she will never be happy again. But God can count our sorrows, which means that even the most horrific grief has limits.

I didn't choose for my brother to take his life. I would have done anything to stop him, but I did not get that choice. God did not abandon my brother, nor did He abandon me and my family on that day.

God is not overwhelmed by my grief and sorrow, but instead, He cares enough to record the moments that I could not pray, the moments that I did not seek Him, and the moments I was alienated in grief. In my darkest night, I was never abandoned nor forsaken. "Even the darkness is not dark to You, And the night is as bright as day," (Psalm 139:12, NASB). I mourn in the shadows and am comforted by the God who lights up the darkness. He is the God who cares for me and for my sorrows.

Hope A. Charters

THE THINGS WE CANNOT SEE

"Now faith is confidence in what we hope for and
assurance about what we do not see."

HEBREWS 11:1 (NEW INTERNATIONAL VERSION)

I was living in Florida where I was a practicing primary care doctor for many years when I learned that my father had become very ill and was hospitalized. I dropped everything to go to North Carolina to be with him. After spending precious time with him for several days, when I thought he was stable and well on the road to recovery, I returned home to care for my Florida patients. Less than twenty-four hours later, my brother called to let me know our dad was critically ill with pneumonia and it did not appear he would survive without aggressive care. But my father had already made his last wishes known, and aggressive care was no part of it. Comfort care was begun and within a few hours, before I could travel back to North Carolina, he had left this earth.

My father and I had a strong bond. He was a dedicated Christian, a loving father and a devoted family man. He had encouraged me to get a good education, to make the most of my time in this life, and to find ways to give back for all the blessings I had received. He and I began having earnest discussions about science and evolution when I was in the tenth grade. I had developed a passionate interest in all things related to science and biology and he was always willing to engage with me on any subject, no matter how little interest he actually may have had in it.

Our father made sure my brothers and I were all raised in the church. I have been a practicing Christian all my life, but if I'm totally honest, before my dad died, in those quiet moments of stark reflection, I had some shadows of doubt about issues that "push the button" of science geeks, like the bodily resurrection of Jesus and life after death. Now, with the shock of my father's death, I had to face these doubts. I simply had not been anticipating my father's passing when I left North Carolina thirty-six hours earlier. And now, I was in a caffeine-fueled adrenaline rush trying to get back to him before he died. My mind was flying in fifty directions at once and I felt I was hanging onto the edge of an emotional cliff. I was praying desperately for God to let my dad live so that I might see him alive one last time. Then, sitting in a car on the way to the airport, I was completely overcome by a sense of peace and calm that mere words are completely insufficient to describe. Somehow I knew my father had passed and I also knew he was with Jesus, he was at peace and no longer in pain. The calm lasted about thirty seconds and then softly faded away like fine dust in the wind. I later discovered that the moment of profound peace was, in fact, the exact time that he passed. Later, my pastor helped me to understand that I had been visited by what he called the Holy Spirit.

I struggle to find the words to explain just how transformational that experience was. After all of our animated discussions about science, it is fascinating to me that the last gift my father gave me was the knowledge that there is a Holy Spirit who is with us always while we are on earth, and that there is peace in the arms of Jesus after this life. My last shards of doubt faded like the dust in the wind.

"Then Jesus told him, 'Because you have seen me, you have believed; blessed are those who have not seen and yet have believed.'" John 20:29 NIV.

Bette Peterson

Bible Study - Photo credit: Sue Lewis

TAUGHT BY TULIPS

When Jesus spoke again to the people, he
said, "I am the light of the world.
Whoever follows me will never walk in
darkness, but will have the light of life."

JOHN 8:12 (NEW INTERNATIONAL VERSION)

Y ou gently pull the cellophane package out of the tall grocery store bucket, examine its colorful contents and walk to the register. Soon, you arrive home with your straight-stemmed, tightly closed flowers, which look like staunch, inflexible, but somehow charming people, all tied up in an enclosed compact bunch.

Since you know they are thirsty, you get a sharp knife and, hoping you don't injure them, you slice off the slightly shriveled end of each perfectly straight stem. Now they look manufactured because you cut all the stems the same length.

Next you fill a wide-mouthed pitcher with fresh water and place the very straight-stemmed, evenly cut, tightly closed blossoms in the water. You ensure that the flowers are displayed evenly spread apart from each other (I think they give a partial sign of relief), and you walk away satisfied.

A day later, if you happen to glance in the direction of the wide-mouthed pitcher, you see the true nature of a tulip on full display. Some stems have stretched taller than others, and each stem is gently, but definitively, bending in a drastically different direction,

89

as though acting anti-social. When you weren't looking, the colorful blossoms opened up and are now dramatically showing their God-given beauty.

"They" say all tulips reach for light. But why, then, is each tulip reaching so vigorously in its own directions? It seems that each is broadcasting its true bent—just like we do. I don't want to stretch the analogy too far, but we all make choices. The light can be shining brightly, yet some of us bend away from it and others of us bend toward it. Some seem to be seeking light and wisdom; some seem to be seeking to hide from the light. The direction we seek determines the light we will find.

Proverbs 14:6 NIV offers us one answer: "The mocker seeks wisdom and finds none, but knowledge comes easily to the discerning."

The apostle John penned an answer Jesus gave: "Light has come into the world, but people loved darkness instead of light because their deeds were evil. Everyone who does evil hates the light, and will not come into the light for fear that their deeds will be exposed. But whoever lives by the truth comes into the light, so that it may be seen plainly that what they have done has been done in the sight of God," John 3:19-21 NIV.

The heart of Jesus is eager for each of His created people to find light in their lifetime. So He made the way perfectly clear in John 8:12 NIV: "When Jesus spoke again to the people, he said, 'I am the light of the world. Whoever follows me will never walk in darkness, but will have the light of life.'"

Let's take our tulip analogy in a very different direction and learn another lesson. What if I put my tulips in a tall narrow-mouthed jar and try to make them all stand very upright? (I think they utter a groan.) This seems totally logical to us since we brought them home with such straight stems. Will they still try to stretch out in varying directions? Yes, it is in their nature to do that! What if these tulips are our children, and what if we create too restrictive an environment around them? Will each child try to stretch and reach? Yes, despite being limited, they will struggle to thrive and struggle to reach God's potential for them. When we put an unnecessarily narrow, tall fence around them, it may be hard for them to even perceive what God made them to be, and what gifts He has blessed them with. They can hardly see over the edge of the tall narrow container to find their uniqueness.

Looking back, I think that in some ways, for some years, this was a picture of me as a mother. Some of the tulips in my "bunch" that I brought home were more vigorous than others. They tried so hard to stretch over the edge of their narrow container that I began to notice. God used those tulips to teach me. I got a new wider container, gave them all fresh water, and they began to thrive beautifully.

Ephesians 6:4 NIV is for both mothers and fathers when it says, "Fathers, do not exasperate your children; instead, bring them up in the training and instruction of the Lord."

This is not a message to give your children a license to be defiant and bend far from God. We are to train them and instruct them. It is a message for us to take note of each individual child's gifts and abilities, fears and personality. Take note, and be willing to adjust your training in light of each tulip being a bit different than the others.

Carol Hill Quirk

GOD'S TIMING, NOT MINE!

*"For in this hope we were saved But hope that is seen is no hope at all.
Who hopes for what they already have? But if we hope for what we
do not yet have, we wait for it patiently."*

ROMANS 8:24-25 (NEW INTERNATIONAL VERSION)

For me, it's hard to wait for, well, just about everything! In
this day of instant gratification, we can have almost anything
we want immediately. With the advances in online shopping,
two days seems too long to wait for something! When I think about
how life was lived hundreds of years ago, it puts this into perspective.
Mail took months to travel; items were often made to order; food
was only delivered if you had out of town guests arriving with it! As
a whole, our society, has become impatient.

It is sometimes taxing to wait for God's timing, even when we
are waiting for something good—going on a mission trip, starting a
job in ministry, leading a small group, marrying that right person,
buying a new car. Doesn't God want every "good thing" and every
"perfect gift" for us sooner rather than later? Trusting in God's
timing means being convinced that He will not allow opportunities
that He intends for us to simply slip by! I have had a lifetime of
making impulsive decisions and then recognizing the hard way that
was not God's path for me. My life is littered with a trail of impatient,
poor decisions and their ugly consequences.

After I trusted my life into the hands of Jesus, I began to
comprehend what God's timing even meant. Then, I learned to pray.

Through mindful and specific prayer, I am able to calm my desire to have everything right now, in my time. Now, I wait patiently for God's time, assured that He is entirely attentive to my needs and pleas. My newfound faith allows me to worry less about things that I cannot control.

My Prayer today is this: Father, I admit it is hard for me to wait for anything. Help me to be patient and trust that you will give me everything I need when I need it. In so many ways, You have helped me through struggles and shown me your faithfulness. Thank you, God, for your undeserved gift of grace and unconditional love.

Linda Hiebert

BLESSED, EVEN IN MOURNING

"Blessed are they who mourn: for they shall be comforted."

MATTHEW 5:4 (ENGLISH STANDARD VERSION)

I t was June 1988, when my mom and I were walking from the parking lot toward the funeral home in NYC. We were going to my Aunt Nanie's wake. My mom and Aunt Nanie were as close as two sisters could be. Not only were they sisters but they worked together too. They literally spent almost every day together! My Aunt Nanie was the matriarch of our family. She was the oldest of seven siblings. She made sure all the holidays took place in her small Bronx apartment and I cannot imagine, even years later, life without my cousins—Marianne, Tricia, Kathy and John.

My mom was quite upset and choking back tears during this short walk and I could not think of anything to say or do that would bring her comfort. My heart broke for her. The only thing I said was, "Ma, you will see her again and you will be together forever one day. You must believe that." I was taught this throughout my school years and believed this to be true.

Years went by and we all figured out ways to go on until my world stopped on May 6, 2005. At that time, my mom was very ill and I spent endless days and nights with her at the hospital. She passed early that May morning. I know it sounds insignificant, but I was upset over losing my watch. The watch had been a birthday gift from my mom, so it meant a lot to me. I looked in the hospital room and asked all who were around us if anyone had seen it, but to no avail. I gathered up all my mom's belongings and placed them in the plastic yellow bin she was given upon her admission. Tears rolled down my face the whole way home as I prayed and asked for a sign so I would know my mom was ok. When I arrived at my home, I juggled everything and accidentally dropped the yellow bin. Low and behold, my watch fell out and landed on my driveway. I looked at the time and it had stopped at 11:20. Later that day, I called my cousin Marianne to tell her about finding my watch and that it had stopped at 11:20. She got very quiet and said, "My mom died at 11:20." All I could think of was that my mom and Aunt Nanie were together again in heaven! Just like I told my mom so many years ago. What a precious gift from God.

Donna Fenty

TRUSTING GOD, NO MATTER WHAT

"Trust in and rely confidently on the Lord with all your heart
And do not rely on your own insight or understanding.
In all your ways know and acknowledge and recognize Him,
And He will make your paths straight and smooth
[removing obstacles that block your way]."

PROVERBS 3:5-6 (AMPLIFIED BIBLE)

I was forty weeks pregnant with our fourth child. Early one morning, I found myself staring at the beautifully decorated crib. I felt as though God was asking me what I would do if I came home to an empty crib? Wow! I pondered the thought and with tears in my eyes, I took a deep breath recalling what we had asked of God, saying "Let this birth be a testimony." I sighed, took another deep breath, and then proposed in my heart to trust in God no matter what. I made a choice not to lean on my own thoughts or understanding but to wholeheartedly put my trust in Him.

Shortly after, the day of our daughter's birth came. There were complications. She went without oxygen for thirty to forty-five minutes. She was pronounced dead after thirty minutes of no heartbeat. The doctor stated, "Terminal, no good!" But, my husband then prayed saying, "In Jesus' Name I speak life into my baby girl." The nurse, who was a believer, picked up a faint heartbeat and encouraged the doctor to continue to work. It was miraculous! After four long hours they were able to stabilize her for a transfer. She was one of five newborns that night who were airlifted for critical care by the Flight for Life team. Our daughter was the most critical, yet she was the only baby to survive. We named her Ariel Christine Lucero, and yes, I went home to an empty crib, but my baby was alive!

Eight weeks later, when we were getting ready for Ariel to be discharged, the doctor approached me and I said, "I noticed Ariel is being sent home without an apnea monitor." I was thinking this was a good thing. But the doctor abruptly said, "It's not going to increase her life expectancy." I was stunned. The doctor took me aside, looked straight into my eyes and said, "Your daughter is not going to live to see her first birthday." I sat very still as I tried to process the information. Then, God reminded me, He is the one to number Ariel's days. Tears began to well up and roll down my face. They were tears of pure joy because I knew in my heart that God was telling me that Ariel was going to live! On April 5, 2022, we celebrated Ariel's 29th birthday.

I wonder how it would have ended had I not trusted in the Lord with all my heart? I'm sure fear would have crippled me. When we operate in fear, we cannot trust. Fear is the opposite of faith. Fear would have sucked the promises of God right out of me. It would have been easy to give in to fear. I chose to step out in faith and I fixed my eyes upon Jesus instead of on fear.

"My heart is fixed, O God, my heart is steadfast and confident! I will sing and make melody"

PSALM 57:7 (AMPLIFIED BIBLE CLASSIC EDITION).

This is one of my favorite Scriptures that continues to get me through difficulties. I hope and pray it will help you too. When your heart is fixed on God and not on the problem, you too, will be able to sing and give the Lord your praises. You will experience the Lord's peace in spite of what you are going through.

I have learned there can be no half-hearted trust. We must trust God wholeheartedly with our entire being. To be able to trust God we must put forth the effort to know Him. The more we know God, the more we will love Him. The more we love Him, the more we will trust Him. When we do, all things become possible. God is always faithful to lead us, to guide us and to bring us through when we trust Him!

I challenge you to plug into God's Word every day to build up your relationship and intimacy with Christ. When you do, and you commit and discipline yourself faithfully, you too will personally be amazed at how wholeheartedly you will begin trusting God no matter what your circumstance is!

Bev Lucero

HIS STILL SMALL VOICE

*"The Lord said, "Go out and stand on the mountain in the
presence of the Lord, for the Lord is about to pass by." Then
a great and powerful wind tore the mountains apart
and shattered the rocks before the Lord, but
the Lord was not in the wind.
After the wind there was an earthquake, but
the Lord was not in the earthquake.
After the earthquake came a fire, but the Lord was not in
the fire. And after the fire came a gentle whisper. When
Elijah heard it, he pulled his cloak over his face
and went out and stood at the mouth of the cave."*

1 KINGS 19:11-13 (NEW INTERNATIONAL VERSION)

Each day there are so many things that scream for our attention. There are jobs to be completed, meals to be prepared, mouths to be fed, cleaning that won't do itself, diapers to be changed (if you are still in that season like me) and quite often there are literal screams for attention from our children. There are so many things that beckon for our attention each day. While many of those things are worthy of our time, we can often find ourselves feeling overwhelmed and weary. In the midst of all of the noise, we crave a moment to press pause and refresh ourselves.

When the Lord told Elijah to stand on the mountain in his presence, the Lord was not in the wind, the earthquake or the fire, but Elijah immediately knew that the sound of the gentle whisper was God's voice. God's leading often comes in the form of a still small voice but we have to find time to slow down and mute all of the other voices so that we can be fully present and listen to Him. So often I find myself living in the beautiful chaos-filled season of raising kids and just making it through the day.

God has been tugging on my heart over the past year and has led my husband and me on a journey to sell our home without knowing where He was leading us. The one thing that I knew for sure was that I was ready to cut out some of the "noise" and simplify in order to focus more fully on Him and His leading. God has walked beside us every step of the way and His presence in even the smallest of details has been so evident.

Hearing God in the noise and the stillness of life demands that we humbly and quietly seek His guidance. I have found that a good test, to help me evaluate whether or not I am humbly in tune with God's leading and truly listening to His still small voice, is to ask myself whether or not I have peace about whatever circumstances I am facing. I have learned that if I am anxious, I may be allowing the windstorm, earthquake, or fires around me to take my focus off of the One who is the giver of every good gift and who has always proven Himself faithful to me and to so many others. When my focus is on Him, I experience the peace that surpasses understanding, but in order to do that I have to stop and listen to His still small voice.

Clare Derbyshire

A PSALM OF DAVID

"Even when I walk through the darkest valley,
I will not be afraid, for you are close beside me.
Your rod and your staff protect and comfort me."

PSALM 23:4 (NEW LIVING TRANSLATION)

God has been with me throughout my life. Sometimes, like a casual friend, I saw Him occasionally, not making enough time for Him. Other times, He was my only friend, and I clung to Him as though my life depended on His protection.

It was September 28, 2000, at six-thirty in the evening, and I had just gotten home after walking Sammy Anne, my basset hound. I was bending down to remove her leash when my world went black. I don't know how, I knew but I knew that I was having a stroke. I laid on the living room floor with my trusted dog and waited three hours for my husband Leo to come home. Time stopped but I knew God was with me, even though I could not move or speak. When Leo arrived and saw me lying on the floor mumbling gibberish, he quickly called for an ambulance and I was soon on the way to the hospital.

A complete sense of calm came over me on the way to the hospital. God had sent an angel to watch over me. I knew that I would survive and be whole again. Unfortunately, the doctors were not as optimistic. They delivered the news to my husband that I had suffered a major catastrophic stroke. A large clot in the left side of my brain caused the right side of my body to be paralyzed. As time passed, the doctors became cautiously optimistic but warned that I may not have use of my right leg or arm.

I was forty-six years old at this time and I was determined I would walk again. Period. The rest of the month was a blur! The days were consumed by physical therapy, speech therapy, and life therapy. This was the first time I depended totally on my left side, working alone, to accomplish tasks for my entire body. Frustration set in as it came to me that this might be my new normal. GOD was with me through my tears.

After receiving care in the hospital, I was brought to a rehabilitation center. For the next month I struggled, still determined to walk on my own again. At times I became discouraged; this was one of those many moments in my life where God was my best friend. I felt His presence.

"This is my command—be strong and courageous! Do not be afraid or discouraged. For the LORD your God is with you wherever you go," Joshua 1:9 NLT.

Thankfully, I survived the rehabilitation center. I will be forever grateful for the supportive and skilled staff. I left the center walking. Though it was with a cane and only a few steps at a time, I was walking! My right arm remained glued to my chest—one down, one to go. I remained strong and grateful.

I eventually returned to work for a few hours a day, thanks to a loving coworker who transported me daily. My wonderful mother moved in with us and cared for me with such love and understanding. My devoted husband continued to be amazing throughout all of the struggles. And most importantly, God was with me as; with His mercy, I continued to defy all odds.

It took over two years for me to drive again. Science finally caught up with me and with Botox injections my arm relaxed to its normal position. Progress! I have known many angels throughout my recovery! And I have learned many lessons.

1. Trust in God... He is strong and merciful, and He is with me.
2. Don't take your life for granted!! It can all change in a moment.
3. Thank those who help you! Take time to help those in need of your help!
4. Be humble! And finally, find joy in your circumstances!

Today I know that I had a stroke to show me things I would not have seen otherwise. It is a "God thing!" Previously my focus was on self and career. Now my focus is on God, confident He is with me, grateful to Him to have survived, able to walk my dog and to love life.

Cindi Kolic

Bird walking on the beach - Photo credit: Bernadette Skipper

LIFE LESSONS IN EVERYDAY LIFE

God is with you whether you believe or not!
"...being confident of this, that he who began a good work in you
will carry it on to completion until the day of Christ Jesus."

PHILIPPIANS 1:6 (NEW INTERNATIONAL VERSION)

Never in my wildest dreams did I realize how God had watched over, protected, and loved me until well into my adult life! I thought my life had been easy without much drama, struggle, or turmoil. Of course, I credited my "easy life" to my ability to make good decisions and great choices. My path was determined by my power, my knowledge, and my skill.

I joined the military straight out of high school at the tender age of eighteen to escape a crowded, low income, crime infested city. Now, as I look back to where I came from as a young woman with no spiritual guidance, I distinctly see God's hand in my entire life!

God gave me the most exceptional, single parent mother who loved, firmly disciplined, and taught me respect for myself and others. Mother sent me to Catholic school from preschool through high school even though she struggled to make the payments. She was not a church goer or practicing believer in Jesus Christ until later in her own life, but she felt strongly that a Christian school was a great place for me to receive a strong academic foundation.

I had been out on my own for quite some time when she gifted me my first Bible. I did not open the Bible until some years later. She would ask me if I had used it yet, and what church was I attending? She repeatedly said the ever so familiar words, "Nothing like experience to teach you a lesson. I can tell you until I'm blue in the face how people are starving in the world, but until you're actually starving, you can't understand. Open your Bible and read it."

I look back on how God allowed my mother to prepare me, though her initial motivation was not a spiritual one. As a young girl growing up in the city and later experiencing military life, I was unaware of the close calls and compromising situations I got myself into time and time again while living life on my terms. God knew that when I escaped bad situations unscathed, I believed my escape was by my own power and cunning. I did not even consider the fact that it was God alongside me all the time! "There but for the grace of God go I," (Old proverb attributed to John Bradford, 1553).

God was preparing me to accept Him into my life, to find His purpose for me, and to live with the help of the Holy Spirit. It takes faith in His word and His promise that life on earth is not our final resting place. We are here, but only for a moment. But while here, we are to love, teach, and point as many hearts upward in His direction as possible and we do this with the help, guidance and nudging of the Holy Spirit. "Therefore go and make disciples of all nations, baptizing them in the name of the Father and of the Son and of the Holy Spirit" Matthew 28:19 NIV. My mom was right; "There is nothing like experience to teach you a lesson." However, everything does not need to be experienced to be believed. You need to have faith in the Lord, you must trust Him, and to know Him intimately, you must read your Bible.

God's word tells us about a man named Jonah who God commanded to bring a vital message to the town of Nineveh. But, "Jonah ran away from the Lord and headed for Tarshish," Jonah 1:3 NIV. As Jonah was escaping to Tarshish, he was swallowed by a big fish. God, the ruler of all, did not permit Jonah's calamity to keep him from carrying out God's plan for Nineveh. I know that my God will enable me to carry out the unique and specific assignment He has for me. I love that my God is that way. We all have our vital part in the body of Christ. Thank you, Jesus, for giving me the privilege to be included in your Kingdom's eternal plan!

Charlotte Simon

DON'T YOU CARE?

*"On that day, when evening came, He said to them, 'Let us go over to
the other side.' Leaving the crowd, they took Him along with them in
the boat, just as He was; and other boats were with Him. And there
arose a fierce gale of wind, and the waves were breaking over the boat
so much that the boat was already filling up. Jesus Himself was in the
stern, asleep on the cushion; and they awoke Him and said to Him,
'Teacher, do You not care that we are perishing?' And He got up and
rebuked the wind and said to the sea, 'Hush, be still.'
And the wind died down and it became perfectly calm."*

MARK 4:35-39 (NEW AMERICAN STANDARD BIBLE 1995)

I t was a gray day, partly from the cloud cover and partly from
pollution. We had lived in this East Asian country for over a
year but many things still seemed foreign. The joy of having our
fifth child here was unforgettable, but the challenges of caring for an
infant and dealing with constant advice from vendors, shop owners
or restaurant patrons whenever we went out had my patience wearing
thin. Our apartment had become too small for us. Two bedrooms
is just not enough for seven people. I found my spirits matching the
color of the sky.

Circumstantially, I was living out the fulfillment of a dream of
raising our family overseas, but my sense of competency was receding
like low tide along the shoreline. While praying, it seemed I had
more questions than answers. In my head I knew the character of
God, His wondrous acts throughout history and even in my past,

and the signs of His activity all around me. But, in my heart I felt like He had put me on hold somehow.

In reading through the fourth chapter of Mark. I found myself in the boat with the fearful disciples. They were being tossed and hurled with the threat of imminent drowning. Their honesty in verse thirty-eight is disarming; "Teacher, do you not care that we are perishing?" They did not say, "Teacher, can't you stop us from perishing?" Like pulling away floorboards to see termite damage, the root of my sorrow was exposed. I was doubting God's intentions toward me. This form of doubt has the ability to erode faith faster than any other. It was deeply comforting to know that I could tell Him how I felt, and it would not offend Him.

In my case, the circumstances did not change much but the Holy Spirit gave me consolation in knowing that I was not alone in my struggle. Jesus did care and does care. This realization ignited my weak faith and nudged me to resolve to look up and not down.

> I will lift up my eyes to the mountains—
> Where does my help come from?
>
> My help comes from the LORD,
> the Maker of heaven and earth.
> Psalm 121:1-2

Is there an area where you are doubting God's care for you? Take some time and confess it to Him and receive His comfort and all-sufficient grace.

Audrey Ogden

MY HEART'S DESIRE

"Delight yourself in the Lord, and He will
give you the desires of your heart."

PSALM 37:4 (MODERN ENGLISH VERSION)

I always imagined I would have a daughter one day. My mom saved all my Barbies, baby dolls and the dollhouse my dad made for me. She even kept a selection of my baby clothes from when I was young. The idea behind it was that one day my own daughter could play with my treasures and how fun it would be to dress up my own little girl in something I once wore as a baby. I was all in too—I always looked forward to the day when I would have my own little girl to love.

The Lord had other plans for me and my husband! He blessed us with three little boys to raise! Even though I am more of a "girly girl" and not so much a "Boy Mom", I absolutely loved each of my sons more than I ever knew was possible. We were hopeful for awhile and tried for a fourth child but it was not to be. I found myself dreaming about sweet daughters-in-law one day. That would fulfill the desire of my heart.

When I was forty-one, my sons were eighteen, sixteen and twelve, my husband and I decided to do something out of the ordinary and give our kids a new cultural experience. We moved our family to Puerto Vallarta, Mexico. It was a big adventure for all of us. Six months after we arrived in Mexico, while enjoying life near the beach, I noticed I was feeling nauseous in the evenings.

On Sunday evening, my husband took the boys to church in Puerto Vallarta. I stayed home since I did not feel well. I decided to get comfy on my bed and read my Bible. Though I rarely read the Psalms, I felt led to read Psalms 37. When I got to verse four, I read "Delight yourself in the Lord, and He will give you the desires of your heart." At that moment I felt the Lord speak to me in my soul and say "You are pregnant and it's a girl." From that moment on, I believed it and never doubted it to be true. That night when my husband got back, I told him I wanted to get a pregnancy test. When the test confirmed my pregnancy we were overjoyed! Everyone who knew us, including our boys, were a bit shocked and delighted!

The boys were at an age they were very helpful to me. It was so good for them to be around a pregnant mom, and then a tiny infant—they learned a lot to tuck away for later when they would one day become husbands and fathers.

I was grateful that I had excellent health care in Mexico and that this was my easiest pregnancy even though I was in my forties. On the day we were to find out if it was indeed a girl...or a boy, it crossed my mind for a single minute that it might be a boy. But then I remembered Psalm 37:4, and I knew the Lord had a girl for me. My doctor said in broken English that he was happy to announce, "It's a Woman!"

Our sweet baby girl was born in August to a Mom and Dad filled with so much love for her. She was blessed to have the best big brothers any little girl could ask for. We named her Graciela for God's wonderful grace to bless us with a daughter so unexpectedly.

Now almost fifteen, our Gracie has spent lots of her younger years enjoying my old dollhouse and other toys from my childhood, I even got to dress her up in my old baby clothes! She has been such a joy to our family.

I share my story to let you know God's timing is not our timing. Sometimes you think your prayer will never be answered or maybe

He just has another plan, but God has the final say. Just keep delighting yourself in the Lord, serving Him and being obedient in the small and large things. He may change your heart's desire or He may give you the desire of your heart.

Jeannie Amaral

YOU FIND WHAT YOU
ARE LOOKING FOR

"Come to me, all you who are weary and
burdened, and I will give you rest."

MATTHEW 11:28 (NEW INTERNATIONAL VERSION)

M any times, I find myself wide awake in the middle of the night. I wonder why chamomile tea, melatonin and other methods of relaxation do not seem to do the trick. In those moments I tend to reflect on all my worries and concerns and then I realize I have a choice to make. Will I seek a loving God who comforts me, or let the weight of the world distract me? Will I allow worldly voices to tell me things are not going to be ok, that I am all alone, and that I am not enough? I have learned that during those moments of worry, I can choose to look to God for comfort and peace and a calm spirit. God's word says, "Come to me, all you who are weary and burdened, and I will give you rest," Matthew 11:28 NIV.

You have a choice to make as well. When you find yourself full of worry you can choose to seek relief from a variety of sources. Let me warn you from experience, choosing poorly can end poorly. What you seek, you will find. When you seek temporary answers, you get temporary answers. When you seek a moment of relief from your struggles through shopping, social media, substances, or whatever your comfort of choice may be, you will get just that. A very brief moment of relief. I challenge you to avoid the short-lived solutions and seek a long-term source of comfort in Jesus. When I give my burdens to God, my stress lightens. "For my yoke is easy, and my burden is light," Matthew 11:30 NIV.

Finally, we have a choice to make when it comes to what we focus on. We can focus on all the bad or we can focus on God's goodness in our lives. When we seek God and make an effort to see what He has done in our past and what He is doing now, our peace grows, and we have thankful hearts that honor Him. I Thessalonians 5:16-18 NIV says: "Rejoice always, pray continually, give thanks in all circumstances; for this is God's will for you in Christ Jesus." When we look for the good in a situation, we acknowledge God's handiwork. We accept God's master plan.

Dear God, help me remember that I find what I am looking for. I can seek your comfort, or I can seek the world's comfort. Help me seek you. Help me see your goodness throughout my life. Help me praise your provisions and help me turn to you with concerns. As I navigate through my day, help me choose you. Amen.

Mykki Cornelius

RECKLESS SURRENDER

"But seek first his kingdom and his righteousness,
and all these things will be given to you as well."

MATTHEW 6:33 (NEW INTERNATIONAL VERSION)

R eckless Surrender: affirming His mighty power through following His revealed truths, one day at a time.

Throughout my spiritual journey, a common message has arisen: "Do You Trust Me?" God has allowed for struggles to come into my path. However, through letting go and trusting Him, these struggles become opportunities.

Often I picture my hands tightly clenched, trying to feel I am in control. However, God tells me to loosen my grip and surrender "everything"—my children, my finances, my relationships, my health, my future—unto Him. It sometimes feels like a free fall and doubt repeatedly creeps in, and I become afraid of crashing. He is using it all to draw me nearer to him as I become hungry for answers, thirsty for comfort, and in need of a loving Father. He is telling me He knows I love Him when things are going well, but will I still praise His name when nothing makes sense, will I still trust Him when the answer is no. He is more concerned with my relationship with Him and not as concerned with my comfort. He knows what I need before I have a clue, and all it requires is for me to unclench my hand.

The Lord keeps reminding me, "For as the heavens are higher than the earth, so are my ways higher than your ways, and my thoughts than your thoughts," Isaiah 55:9 KJV. He questions me, "Do you trust me?" Then His word reminds me, "But seek first his kingdom and his righteousness, and all these things will be given to you as well," Matthew 6:33 NIV.

As we let go, we also have a job to do. We are blessed to be his servant, to give our tithes, to use our talents, to be generous with others. "Give, and you will receive. Your gift will return to you in full—pressed down, shaken together to make room for more, running over, and poured into your lap. The amount you give will determine the amount you get back," Luke 6:38 NLT. Then He supplies—He is our provider, our restorer, our counselor, and our good Father in every crisis.

As Christ followers, we are taught to live differently from the world. The world's mindset is to self-gratify, to be in control, to climb the ladder of success, and to impress people. Yet the Word says, "Do nothing from rivalry or conceit, but in humility count others more significant than yourselves. Let each of you look not only to his own interests, but also to the interests of others. Have this mind among yourselves, which is yours in Christ Jesus," Philippians 2:3-5 ESVUK.

Every day is a challenge to submit to His ways. This is how we grow stronger spiritually. Submitting to His will is an exercise to transform us into His image. So why do I call this devotional, "Reckless Surrender"? The world would call this concept nonsense, but God says, "Casting all your care upon Him; for He cares for you," I Peter 5:7 NKJV. In other words, "SURRENDER ALL."

Lydia Prussel

THE IMPORTANCE OF "SPOTTING"

"I lift up my eyes to you, to you who sit enthroned in heaven."

PSALM 123:1 (NEW INTERNATIONAL VERSION)

In gymnastics and other sports, it is important to keep your eyes on a certain spot. The term athletes use is "spotting." Spotting is finding a fixed focal point in front of you for your eyes to lock onto in order to stay steady in a certain place. Where we focus our eyes can be important in many aspects of life.

The year my daughters Joanna and Christina turned nine and seven, an outdoor trampoline was their birthday wish. My husband and I decided to purchase one for them. One Saturday morning, with the girls supervising every move, we assembled it in our backyard. Christina was first on, and she quickly began laughing, shouting with joy and jumping.

When Joanna's turn came she began taking small tentative jumps. As she gained confidence she began to jump higher, but when she did so, she began to lose control.

She started getting dangerously close to the edge and she stopped. "I can't do this Mommy! I can't stay in the middle. I'm afraid I'm going to fall."

"Stay right there," I answered. I ran into the house, grabbed a sheet of paper and drew a large dot in the middle. Then I taped it to the house in front of the trampoline and I told her, "When you jump, look at the dot. If you do, you will stay in the middle." Her frightened look was replaced with confidence as she steadily jumped in the middle. She had learned the importance of spotting!

A wonderful Biblical illustration about spotting is found in Matthew 14:22-31. Jesus told His disciples to get in a boat and cross the Sea of Galilee but a great storm hit in the middle of the night. Jesus began walking on the water towards the disciple's boat but they were frightened, thinking He was a ghost.

When Jesus identified Himself, Peter spoke out boldly, "Lord, if it's you...tell me to come to you on the water." Jesus then replied, "Come." Peter got out of the boat and began to walk on the water toward Jesus. But when Peter noticed the wind and waves, he began to sink and he cried out for the Lord to save him. As long as Peter kept his eyes on Jesus, he stayed above the waves but, when he took his eyes off Jesus, he was overwhelmed, he lost his faith and began to sink. Yet he did not sink so deep that Jesus could not grab hold of his hand and save him.

We live in a stormy world. Waves of problems—emotional upheaval, financial stress, relationship and family issues, illness—can threaten to pull us under. If we focus on our storms, they overwhelm and overpower us. But if we choose to focus on Jesus, He has the power to keep us above life's storms.

How do we do it?

> Stay connected to God through his Word, where His promises help keep us steady.

> Stay focused on Him through our worship, praising Him for who He is in our lives.

> Stay focused by understanding how He is the provider of all things.

> Stay focused by remembering that God is greater than any circumstance.

If we keep our eyes on Jesus, we won't miss out on all that God has for our lives. "Spotting" on Jesus will allow us to have an extraordinary walk with Him every day.

Angela Catalano

Flooded Boardwalk - Photo credit: Sue Lewis

LESSONS FROM THE LITTLES

"Jesus said, "Let the little children come to me, and do not hinder them, for the kingdom of heaven belongs to such as these."

MATTHEW 19:14 (NEW INTERNATIONAL VERSION)

"**O**ut of the mouths of babes," I think that is how the expression goes. Now that my daughter CK is three, some of her expressions, "CK-isoms", are pretty priceless. Below are a few of my favorites.

CK says "anicorn" for unicorn and "Fancy Fancy" for the Disney show "Fancy Nancy." She admonishes me by saying, "Come on Mom, get it to-ge-ber." Her dad's favorite expression is "I don't like that good idea."

CK has been using her "I don't like that good idea" for some time now. In a conversation with my Bible Study Fellowship, I told them about a day that we were running late and I was trying to get CK to put her shoes on. She told me, "Mommy I don't like that good idea." I wanted her to wear sensible shoes and she wanted to wear light up Cinderella shoes. At the end of my anecdote, one of the much wiser women of my group said, "Aren't we just like that sweet baby telling God that we don't like His good idea by how we live all the time?"

There it was, in my face—our human nature and sin wrapped up in one little phrase. What my three year old is telling me is what I am screaming at God when I choose disobedience. I am no different than a two-year-old throwing a fit when I tell God I don't want to do what He says because, "I don't like that good idea!"

If I am honest, I know deep down that God's way, His "good idea", is way better than whatever I want to do. But like little CK, I want my way. I want my "bad idea" more. I try to dress it up in a "fancy-fancy" way with excuses or compromises or flowery terms. In reality each time I choose my way I am telling God, "I don't like Your good idea."

Like all three-year-olds, CK has a variety of reasons for not liking her parent's good ideas. When I'm about to lose my patience with her, sometimes I hear God whisper, "Mere, do you get it? My good idea could have helped you avoid…." Or I hear, "Mere, see the mess you could have avoided if you had yielded to My 'good idea'?"

Sometimes our children think we are "mean" when we are simply looking out for them. Being a parent has helped me realize that God is just looking out for me when he calls me to a plan I don't understand and don't really want to follow. I hear him whisper, "Mere, I am looking out for you because I am GOD and I know better than you. I LOVE and ADORE you! You are one of my greatest treasures!"

And again, there it is—the gospel, my only hope, summed up in a lesson taught to me by my three-year-old.

Meredith Bennett Rae

WHAT'S LOVE GOT TO DO WITH IT?

"God is love. When we take up permanent residence in a life of love,
we live in God and God lives in us. This way, love has the run of the
house, becomes at home and mature in us, so that we're free of worry
on Judgment Day—our standing in the world is identical with Christ's.
There is no room in love for fear.
Well-formed love banishes fear. Since fear is crippling, a fearful life—
fear of death, fear of judgment—is one not yet fully formed in love."

1 JOHN 4: 17-18 (THE MESSAGE)

"Well-formed love, BANISHES fear." Did you catch that? Other Bible translations call this love that banishes fear "perfect love." What is this fear that is conquered by love? Merriam-Webster defines fear as "an unpleasant, often strong emotion, caused by anticipation or awareness of danger." The Bible says well-formed or perfect love keeps fear out of our lives! Let's stop and think. Has there been a day when not one bit of fear invaded your thoughts? The idea of never having fear seemed far-fetched because I did not understand the authority and power of God's love in my own life.

I tried to identify some real fears like the ones that keep me up at night. The top three were: fear of judgment, fear of death, and fear of the unknown. How can LOVE conquer those fears? That is when it hit me. God knows our story and He knows our entire life. Nothing that happens to us surprises Him. It's not that we will enjoy every moment of our life, nor will life as a Christ follower be easy.

However, God loves us through it all. His perfect love will be with us through the judgment from others, through death, and through the unknown future that lays before us.

Living in God's perfect well-formed love is not something that comes overnight. It may be a daily battle to rely on God's love to get you through day-to-day trials and fears. As we rely on God's love, we are called to share God's love with others, extending grace, not judgment. I John 4:7-20 teaches us that love is the strongest tool God has given us. Use HIS love in your own life and share it in the lives of others!

"Above all, clothe yourselves with love, which binds us all together in perfect harmony." Colossians 3:14, NLT

Christine Abad

RENEW YOUR MIND AND GUARD YOUR HEART

"Do not conform to the pattern of this world, but be transformed by the renewing of your mind. Then you will be able to test and approve what God's will is—his good, pleasing and perfect will."

ROMANS 12:2 (NEW INTERNATIONAL VERSION)

"Above all else, guard your heart, for everything you do flows from it."

PROVERBS 4:23 NIV

God tells us in His word that the things we allow into our minds and hearts matter. There are so many avenues for information and content to come into our minds and hearts these days so we must stay diligent and purposely choose what we allow in. From TV and movies to music and podcasts, books and social media to the company we keep, there are endless paths to our hearts and minds. The things of this world will often bombard us but we have the power through the Holy Spirit to choose life-giving content. We can delete, unfollow, and turn off content that is not life-giving so we are not "conforming to the pattern of this world." We can be "transformed" and renew our minds by seeking more of God in His presence and in His Word.

In Proverbs we are told to guard our heart because everything we do flows from it. Wow, that not only impacts us but those around us too. What we have in our heart seeps out into our lives and spills over to everyone we interact with. Think of the impact we can have

125

on others if we fill our hearts with things of God—things like love, peace, grace, mercy, kindness, patience or joy. Surely our life and those we interact with will be greatly impacted for Jesus!

The New Living Translation of Proverbs 4:23 says, "Guard your heart above all else, for it determines the course of your life." Ponder that! Truly guarding our hearts has an impact on the direction of our life.

Would you pray with me?

"Father, thank you for your Word and your presence in my life. God, would you strengthen me to make any changes in my life to better align with your Word? Please help me to determine what content is not healthy for my mind and heart. Would you draw me in and give me the desire to spend time with you in your Word? If I am unaware of some sin, convict my heart to change. Thank you God that I don't have to clean myself up before I can come to you Lord, but rather you meet me where I am. Please help me to renew my mind and guard my heart as you tell us in your Word in your Son Jesus' name.

Lindsey DeWitt

LET GOD BE GOD

"The Lord will fight for you; you need only to be still."

————————

EXODUS 14:14 (NEW INTERNATIONAL VERSION)

O nce caught in the midst of the rush of life's activities, I found myself constantly moving faster…and faster…and faster… and faster. On any particular day, or in any particular hour, I would seamlessly transition from wife to mom, to friend, to trainer, and back again, all at a moment's notice.

As I attempted to share kindness, empathy, and encouragement with those whose paths I may have crossed, I was experiencing something else within. My own heart was pounding, aching, and sometimes even breaking, and my personal thoughts were running on like never ending stories.

Until that moment—that single event, that one thing that happened—which caused the momentum to STOP. It was at that moment that I came to realize just how hard I had been fighting, just how fast I had been running, and just how long I had been striving to be everything for everyone. I had longed to love and to be loved, while endlessly searching for answers beyond my understanding. But it was also in that moment that I learned to be still.

For the Lord, in His abundant grace, led me to Exodus 14:14, to remind me that He was fighting for me, I needed only to be still. No action required, no worry needed, no plan to be proposed. He is fighting for me, I need only to be still.

Now, I cherish those moments of stillness.

In the midst of the rush of life's activities, I pause with confidence, knowing that He will be fighting for me. I take a deep breath and let God be God.

Leah J Riggenbach

LOSS—A NEW PERSPECTIVE BRINGS GRATITUDE

"The LORD gave and the LORD has taken away. Blessed be the name of the LORD."

JOB 1:21B (NEW AMERICAN STANDARD)

B y my late sixties, I had experienced the loss of many close family members and cherished friends. Some had lived many wonderful years and their passing felt natural. I still miss them terribly, but I celebrate their lives rather than focus on their loss. However, I carried intense pain and deep hurt for years after my Father died.

I was a new Christian in my late twenties when my father became very sick. My mom took him to a care facility a few hours from home. After they arrived at the facility, I spoke to Dad on the phone to let him know I would visit him that weekend. In the meantime, I was working feverishly to finish a pen and ink drawing of a quaint town on an island off the coast of New England. Dad had sent me a photo of the scene months earlier, knowing I would love its rustic beauty. I was eager to show him the completed drawing before he was gone.

The next day I received a phone call from a kind elderly Christian man who had heard of my Dad's condition and wanted to visit him to share the gospel. I was so hopeful that God would grant my dad ears to hear the simple message of salvation and peace in Christ. The following evening the phone rang and it was my mom with the heart-wrenching news that Dad had died. That was the day before the elderly man was to have visited him. Desperate confusion took over my soul. Why had God arranged such a special meeting and then brought death before He brought the new life I had prayed for? Why had he died before I got there to say goodbye? Why did he have to die alone? My only hope is that God dealt with my Dad as he lay alone in his room in those dying hours, convincing him of the truths I had spoken to him years before. I knew that my God was just and merciful, but for years, I questioned if He answered my prayers.

Many years later in my early sixties, I was recovering from my second war with lymphoma. It was winter when we left the treatment center in New York City to return to our country home upstate. I was spending my days by the fireplace, trying to keep my bony body warm, when I received a text from my younger sister announcing that she finally purchased a smartphone. So, we set up a FaceTime call for later that day. It was mid-afternoon when I settled into a sunny spot on an upstairs bed and we chatted happily like teenagers, enjoying each other's smiles. When I heard her doorbell ring, she said, "Gotta go!" I casually said, "See ya', love you." That was our only FaceTime call. The next evening her husband called. Twenty four hours after our call, she had gone from the arms of her husband to the arms of Jesus. She had been battling metastatic breast cancer.

Though I felt the huge loss of someone with whom I had shared a lifetime of joy, I soon realized that God's hand had given me an incredible gift the day before. I celebrated that gift as I mourned the loss, with no resentment or questioning of God's providence. This girl who captured the beauty of God's creation with her camera was now seeing the incredible beauty of her Lord.

With the loss of my sister, my perspectives had changed and my confidence in God had grown. I was finally able to replace the pain and hurt of the loss of my father with overflowing gratitude. I realized that even a limited number of years with a good father were years to be celebrated. In those years, he had given me a solid foundation in life. He had modeled faithfulness, kindness, creativity, diligence and goodness. My focus turned to what God had given me, and not what He had taken away from me. Deep gratitude replaced pain and hurt.

Carol Quirk

MIRACLES STILL HAPPEN

"But it was your own eyes that saw all these great things the Lord has done."

DEUTERONOMY 11:7 (NEW INTERNATIONAL VERSION)

December 2019 was the beginning of an extremely tough time for our family. My adult son became extremely sick. We were called to go to his hospital room to say our goodbyes to him. My first thought was not to pray but to get up there to take care of whatever was going on.

When we arrived, we stared at our unresponsive son as the minutes passed. I finally started to cry out to God to save my son. It was a desperately difficult and painful time for me, but I have never felt closer to the Lord than I did in those moments. I have never prayed so hard for anything in my life. I was experiencing every emotion you could imagine while watching my son lie there, not knowing if he was going to live or not. Jesus put His arms around me and held me tighter than I have ever been held.

As I look back, I can see that the best is yet to come. Even though God did not heal my son according to how our family prayed, God healed him in His way for His glory.

Through the darkest time of my life, I have never felt the power of prayer like I did in those moments. People all over the world were praying for my son and our family. I felt every one of those prayers. Now I understand what intercessory prayer is, what it feels like, and how vital it is.

My prayer was not answered the way I desired, but it was answered. It was answered the way God wanted it to be, in His way and in His timing. God does not say our lives will be without trials. It is how we manage those trials that shows who we are and how much we really trust our God. Our family truly witnessed miracles happen on an hourly basis as we all went through this trial. I can tell you that miracles still happen, and that God is still good.

God has given our son amazing grace through this entire process. God's enabled him to face these trials bravely and he is now motivating others to face their trials and struggles. God has given him a platform where he shares God's goodness and where he gives God all of the glory. "I have told you these things, so that in me you may have peace. In this world you will have trouble. But take heart! I have overcome the world"

John 16:33 NIV.

Linda Miracle

Brevard Zoo - Photo credit: Linda Foster

FAITH

"For I am convinced that neither death nor life, neither angels nor demons, neither the present nor the future, nor any powers, neither height nor depth, nor anything else in all creation, will be able to separate us from the love of God that is in Christ Jesus our Lord."

ROMANS 8:38-39 (NEW INTERNATIONAL VERSION)

That passage from God's word WOWS me every time I read it. My mother and I shared this as our most favorite passage in the Bible. It encapsulated the foundation of her beliefs that she passed on to me.

How powerful is it to know these words of Paul are true for us as believers. No one gets through this life without challenges, pains, tribulations and trials of all kinds. But, there is not and never will be any challenge in my life I cannot overcome with God at my side.

It doesn't matter how severely Satan is testing me, God is always with me! We never know when Satan may sneak up from behind and attack when we are unprepared. And we never know when he may try to take us down even while we are looking him in the eye. But, there is absolutely nothing in all the universe that can separate us from God's love. There is no place on the planet where we can be placed that He is not at our side. There is no challenge I cannot overcome. There is no burden I cannot bear.

Each time I read this verse, it takes my breath away. What comfort that knowledge provides. What strength that belief provides. What difficult times that verse has pulled me through.

So...WOW! I know beyond a doubt that nothing ever can separate me from God's love. It is the solid rock on which I stand—the foundation on which I live my life.

Bette Peterson

GOD'S MASTERPIECE

"For we are His workmanship, created in Christ Jesus for good works,
which God prepared beforehand that we should walk in them."

EPHESIANS 2:10 (NEW KING JAMES VERSION)

How we view ourselves has a lot to do with how we live, the choices we make, and the thoughts we think. Our mind is the control center of our thoughts, so we must be careful stewards of what resides there. What we allow to dwell in our minds has a direct effect on how we feel and how we act which impacts our overall well-being. We choose our "thought life."

Why is this worthy of consideration? Our minds can process thousands of thoughts in one day from a myriad of sources: what we see, what we hear, what we've been told, what the culture says, what our past replays, and what the enemy of God whispers to us. If we can learn to identify our thoughts as truth or lies, we can discard the lies and dwell on the truths. If we can align our thoughts with God's view, then we will see ourselves, our world, and others in such a way as to experience a transformed life. The good news is that God has equipped us with everything we need to accomplish the renewing of our minds. We have His complete infallible Word, the Bible, and His Holy Spirit living in our hearts to guide us in all truth.

Let us consider this one thought. Did you know that you are God's "workmanship?" Some translators use the word, "masterpiece." This means you are God's work of art, His handiwork, His greatest creation! Pause and let it sink in. You are not a mistake. There are

137

no flaws He can not redeem and make new—even your brokenness. Your life story has been prepared since before the day you were born. Walk in the goodness of His promises and be conformed to His image, His fingerprint. An unfolding masterpiece, that is what you are!

Does that one life-giving, transforming, divine truth take up proper residence in your thought life? Remember, you get to choose. Your Creator, the Sovereign God of the universe who spoke everything you see into existence, has put in place every part of your life as His crowning achievement. He never fails. He finishes what He starts. "Being confident of this very thing, that He who has begun a good work in you will complete it until the day of Jesus Christ," Philippians 1:6 NKJV.

Oh, how God is looking for surrendered hearts and minds in His daughters for these glorious promises to be lived out in today's culture. Just look around. People are desperately looking for hope, significance, and purpose. In Christ, you are rich in mercy and grace and He has provided you with truth!

Consider these next steps:

• Decide daily that you will live like God's beloved masterpiece!
• Draw near to Him through the study of His Word.
• Quiet your mind and look for opportunities He brings across your path.
• Surrender the cares of this world and embrace His power to accomplish supernatural things.
• Trust Him to use you in a powerful way to make an impact.
• Live in the abundance of His ways, His purposes, and the deep fulfillment it brings.

To God be the glory forever and always!

Kim Wheeler

CHOSEN

"I chose you. I appointed you to go and produce fruit"

JOHN 15:16B (CHRISTIAN STANDARD BIBLE)

W e remember it all too well, waiting on the sidelines while the team captains picked their teams for kickball. It felt like forever as one by one, the biggest and strongest were chosen first, followed by the most beautiful or popular. If you were small in stature or one of the marginalized, you were usually among the handful of those last chosen.

When Jesus came to earth, He turned the world upside down! He said the last will be first and the first will be last, (Matthew 20:16). Jesus chose you! God lovingly chooses the last and the first, the outcast and the popular, the beautiful and the awkward, the foolish and the educated, the popular and the marginalized. He came to rescue and redeem ALL people. God loves us so much that He gave His only Son for our salvation, (John 3:16). Jesus came to bind up the broken hearted, to set the captives free from the bondage of sin, to turn our mourning into rejoicing, and give us life abundantly in Him, (Isaiah 61:1-4, John 10:10). Jesus continually emphasized that all people are created equal, regardless of ethnicity, social class, or gender, (Galatians 3:28). God created ALL human beings with great worth and value; we are made in His image, (Genesis 1:27, Psalm 139). Therefore, we want to show God's love to everyone!

God created us as His beautiful masterpiece, "For we are his workmanship, created in Christ Jesus for good works, which God prepared ahead of time for us to do," (Ephesians 2:10). This is incredible! We are literally God's work of art, and He has already planned the good works He wants us to do. We simply need to step forward in obedience and follow His lead.

When observing another human being, we can look past their outward appearance and love the inner person God created them to be. Sometimes this can be difficult when some people are not walking the path God created them to walk in. Instead, they are following meaningless pleasures resulting in their mind and body becoming decrepit and wasting away. Often, they look like the walking dead, hallowed shells of people. Our hearts break over them. When we see one of God's creatures wasting away in this manner, this often prompts us to get on our knees and pray for them.

To intercede for someone means to go between God and man through prayer, conveying the needs of poor and broken people to our rich and mighty God. We can lovingly intercede for others because as Christians, "God's love has been poured out in our hearts through the Holy Spirit who was given to us," (Romans 5:5).

God chose you!! He loves you more than you could possibly imagine! You are not left last on the sidelines of the kickball team. He's calling you to be in the game! Let's be ALL IN!

"We can be in our day what the heroes of faith were in their day – but remember at the time they didn't know they were heroes." -A.W. Tozer

Let's look for the marginalized and for ways to bless them. Let's pray for the people whom, God places in our path today. God wants to use you!

Harmony Charters

HE IS JEALOUS FOR YOU

"For you shall not worship any other god, because the LORD, whose name is Jealous, is a jealous God"

EXODUS 34:14 (NEW AMERICAN STANDARD BIBLE)

A few years ago, my six-year-old daughter got to go on a special date with her daddy. To say she was excited would be a grand understatement! She was elated at the thought of getting dressed up like a princess. For three weeks, she would daily ask, "How many more days till my date with daddy?" Her excitement was well justified, for this wasn't just "any date"—she was preparing for the kind of evening that every little girl (and most grown women) fantasizes about! The activities for the evening were planned by our fabulous church and included a limo ride to the Melting Pot for chocolate fondue.

My husband played the part of Prince Charming fantastically. He picked out an outfit that coordinated with hers and gladly joined in on the fun! With four young kids in our home, one on one time was quite rare, so he was genuinely anxious and excited about spending some devoted time talking with his six-year-old! When they joined the group of girls and their daughters at church, almost immediately he discovered that when surrounded with a group of giggly, giddy girls her attention was divided! She easily gravitated towards comparing shoes and necklaces and sharing lip gloss with her church girlfriends instead of basking in the individual attention of her father. As a result, my husband came home slightly disappointed because he felt he never really got to connect with her. He longed to ask her about school, friends, and new likes and dislikes. Instead, he found himself a bystander most of the evening, watching her enjoy the company of her friends on his "special evening" with her.

As I thought about this scenario, I was reminded of the infinitely amplified jealousy that the Bible describes God as having for us, His children. I wonder if what my husband felt is a small glimpse of how God often feels about what happens in churches every week. Our Father watches us get dressed in our Sunday best with coordinated jewelry and shoes. We carefully apply our make-up, fix our hair, and we rush to church for our set aside "date" with Him. Yet, how easily our attention is divided, and we are lured away from His presence. Our thoughts are cluttered. Our hearts are hardened to messages that are too convicting or personal. We are distracted by to-do lists, regrets from last week or anxiety for the week ahead. Can we be honest enough to admit that sometimes as Christians we "do church" socially and enjoy laughing and chatting with friends more than connecting intimately with the heart of God?

Exodus 34:14 says, "You must worship no other gods, for the LORD, whose very name is Jealous, is a God who is jealous about his relationship with you."

God wants our attention and sole devotion not because His ego needs it, and certainly not because we have anything unique to offer Him, but because He loves us! He is zealous about us and is jealous about His relationship with us individually. Isn't it mind boggling that the God who made the universe wants to be so intimately acquainted with you personally that He would be jealous when your attention is divided?

God's invitation for each of us is that of a sacred romance between only two. You and Him. He longs to speak to your individual circumstances, to share joyfully in your successes, to comfort your heartache and to empathize with your frustrations. He faithfully waits to grant you wisdom in your times of confusion and to grant you clarity in your difficult decisions. He holds in confidence your secret dreams, your passions, and the desires of your heart.

God invites us to call him "Abba Father." Literally, He says, "Call me Daddy!" He wants to know us intimately, as a devoted father knows his child. Our Daddy's loving offer is a daily invitation into the wondrous joy of His presence!

Jealousy is an intense emotion, often with negative implications. God's jealousy, however, is rooted in a passionate love, and should make us feel secure and protected in our covenant relationship with Him. As demonstrated over and over again in the story of the Israelites and their repeated unfaithfulness, God's heart broke when His people wandered away from Him. He always sought to woo them back into a love relationship exclusively with Him as their first love.

God is jealous for you. Not for your talents. Not for your money, or anything you can do, give, or earn. He is jealous for you because He knows and wants what's best for you. He understands the longings of your heart and He alone knows how to fill the God-shaped hole within each of us.

Christina Stolaas

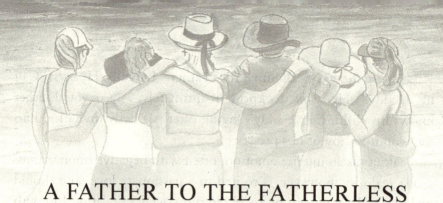

A FATHER TO THE FATHERLESS

"A father of the fatherless, a defender of widows, is God in His holy habitation. God sets the solitary in families; He brings out those who are bound into prosperity."

PSALM 68:5-6 (NEW KING JAMES VERSION)

I was eleven years old when my father, well I thought he was my father, left my mother with seven children. He left us for another woman and he started a new family. We were crushed and filled with hurt and anger. When he left us, it triggered my struggle with fear and anxiety that I still wrestle with. I grew up with no self-esteem. I no longer trusted people, especially men. I made the decision that I did not want to have children in this cruel world. Then, at the age of eighteen, my mother told me that the only father I knew was not my biological father, and that my biological father did not want me. That knowledge caused more hurt.

But Jesus in all His glory placed loving Christian families in my life. He gave me spiritual parents that loved and discipled me. They helped me to change my old way of thinking to God's way of thinking and to have a new attitude in Christ.

"So Jesus answered and said, 'Assuredly, I say to you, there is no one who has left house or brothers or sisters or father or mother or wife or children or lands, for My sake and the gospel's, who shall not receive a hundredfold now in this time—houses and brothers and sisters and mothers and children and lands, with persecutions—and in the age to come, eternal life,'" Mark 10:29-30 NKJV.

Sherette T. Filmore

WORK FOR THE LORD

"Whatever you do, work heartily, as for the Lord and not for men,"

COLOSSIANS 3:23 (ENGLISH STANDARD VERSION)

I was tired. I was heading to work for my third twelve-hour shift in as many days. It seemed as if I had just left the unit and here I was on my way back. I'm a nurse in an Intensive Care Unit and I knew what, or rather who, awaited me there. I put on the uplifting Christian radio station and prayed for the Holy Spirit to quickly impart the fruits of the Spirit to me. I knew I was in dire need of patience, kindness, goodness, and self-control.

Checking the assignment board, I was not surprised to see I had the same patients as the prior two days. Great, another shift caring for Bed #16 or, as my co-workers referred to him, "Mr. Difficult." Par for the course, #16's visitors were demanding and needy as well.

Holy Spirit, please hurry!

Throughout my shift, I managed #16's complex post-operative recovery, found "Gunsmoke" on the television, located the only orange jello left in the entire hospital, answered the call bell numerous times, fluffed pillows, added ice to water, got new water because previous water was too cold, provided blankets from the warmer, removed blankets when he was too warm, answered a million questions, reminded visitors they weren't supposed to use the patient's bathroom, opened the blinds, closed the blinds, got him up to a chair, put him back to bed, raised the head of the bed, lowered it, reviewed countless medications, got him a deck of cards from the break room, explained what the numbers on the monitor meant, and listened to his wife's explanation of pinochle. I could go on! Only by the grace of God was I able to put a smile on my face and provide care to #16 as if he were my own dad. My shift ended without incident, and I said good-bye to my patients—maybe part of me was thinking good riddance #16.

Fast forward to several weeks later. My nurse manager called me into his office and informed me that I would be receiving a "Daisy Award" for the past quarter. Nurses are nominated by anyone in the organization—patients, family members, other nurses, physicians, other clinicians and staff,—anyone who experiences or observes extraordinary compassionate care being provided by a nurse. I was humbled and honored. But who nominated me? As the letter was read, it became clear that it was from #16! He recounted many of the "things I did" and how I "went out of my way" to help him recover. He even mentioned he probably wasn't the "nicest patient"! I still have his hand written letter.

Colossians 3:23 helped me that day and continues to guide my actions on a daily basis. When I'm frustrated, annoyed, troubled, tired, or insensitive during my workday, I remember that I am "working as for the Lord, and not for men." What a blessing it is to be in relationship with the God of the universe, who sees us, and acknowledges our obedience in ways that never fail to humble and inspire.

The Holy Spirit did answer my cry to hurry to my side. He gave me grace to act in love as Jesus commanded us to do.

Carol Burgunder

MORE FAITH PLEASE!

"And without faith it is impossible to please God, because anyone who comes to him must believe that he exists and that he rewards those who earnestly seek him."

HEBREWS 11:6 (NEW INTERNATIONAL VERSION)

I've spent a lot of my life being a "people pleaser." At work, in the home, with my friendships and my family. It seemed to me that to gain approval I needed to do things that made me look good to others. My pride didn't understand that every good thing I did was not necessarily from me, but a gift from God. I owe every success to a God that has blessed me throughout my life but has also sustained me through some really hard struggles as well.

Once I became a born-again Christian, I realized that this "people-pleasing" attitude was the way I approached God as well. I exerted great effort to do the right things that I thought would please him so that I would find favor in his eyes. I really didn't understand what **faith** meant. I started studying the Bible and the Scriptures with my newly found women's small group at my new church, yep, you guessed it, Church at Viera. I was amazed that I had lived most of my life thinking I knew what being a God-fearing Christian was, and usually getting it all wrong. The Bible says it is impossible to please God without faith. What is faith I asked? Hebrews 11:1 ESV gives us one of the best biblical definitions of faith - *"Now faith is the assurance of things hoped for, the conviction of things not seen."* I finally realized that it is not what I do that will please God; it is having a heart that seeks to follow him, in times of joy and in times of struggle and sorrow.

My absolute faith in God and his promises turned that people-pleaser heart into a servant's heart. I am more confident in my approach to others, and I don't need to worry about what others think of me or seek their approval. I now try to serve others humbly, without regard to how others may see me or what that earthly reward might look like. I know that my God is pleased with me, not because of what I do, but because of what I believe!

My prayer today is this: Heavenly Father, I come with a heart that wants to please only you. Forgive me for thinking that all the good things I do are more important than a heart that believes in you and continually seeks your will. I have faith in you alone. You hear my prayers and even if I cannot see your response, I know that you are working, and will wait patiently for my heavenly reward of seeking you.

Linda Hiebert